magic sponge

This book is dedicated to Alex Noone

Printed in the United Kingdom
First Printing, 2020

3 Dean Trench Street
Westminster
London, SW1P 3HB
www.Q5Partners.com

A collection of interviews with inspiring business leaders from 2010–2020, from their tips and techniques to their magic and baggage

magic sponge

OLLY PURNELL & ANDY COTTRILL

Interviewers

Nb. The following initials denote who conducted each interview
CC: Chris Conder
AC: Andy Cottrill
DE: Daryl Edwards
JG: Jen Gramolt
TL: Tom Leary
CP: Chris Parsons
OP: Olly Purnell
SR-O: Sharon Rice-Oxley
DU: Dan Upward

Contents

Foreword

The business world is full of extraordinary people who come in all shapes and sizes, each with their own unique approach to leadership. Every one of them in turn will have been influenced over the course of their careers by those that they have grown up with and worked alongside. They have been shaped by the situations that they have encountered and the challenges they have navigated to become who they are today. From 'benevolent despots' to 'rational consensualists' (and everything above, beyond and in-between) boardrooms the world over are populated by a remarkable range of differing leadership styles.

Magic Sponge has been a labour of love for Olly Purnell (Managing Partner at Q5). Leaving to one side the fascinating and important work that his firm does, I'm not surprised that he and his team have produced a book of this sort. They have a passion for people and a deep and long-standing interest in the psychology of businesses. They have known and worked closely with so many business leaders, stepping into their worlds, that they're brilliantly positioned to be a conduit into their stories.

The relationships and trust they have built and the insights they have uncovered are beautifully demonstrated by this book. It contains a range of interviews, from leaders of some of the most influential brands in the world, to entrepreneurs who have bet their homes on the firms that they have founded. Some of the organisations that they represent have hundreds of thousands of employees, whilst others are family-run concerns with a handful of people.

Each interview is conducted in a respectful, conversational style, gently probing the experiences that helped shaped their approach. Each conversation offers a glimpse of what each leader was facing at a specific point in time during the 2010s. It doesn't shy away from some of the challenges and anxieties that they have confronted but offers a candid firsthand perspective from the captains on the bridge. I know some of the people who feature in this book and whilst all have tasted considerable success during their careers, a few have also stared into the abyss. As ever, there is so much one can learn from their experiences of both.

Magic Sponge is therefore an apt title for this anthology. Absorb what you can!

Charles Gurassa
Chair, Channel 4
Trustee of English Heritage & the Migration Museum
April 2020

Introduction

No-one grows up wanting to be a management consultant. Ask one why they chose their line of work and you'll usually get one of two answers: 'I didn't know what I wanted to do, and this seemed vague enough', or 'for the variety and interest of work'.

It's the latter of these that sowed the seed for this volume of interviews: not only do you get to do a huge variety of work as a consultant, but you meet a lot of interesting people along the way.

This book is a collection of interviews with some of the outstanding people we have met at Q5, during the 2010s. It is made up of a mixture of clients, friends and heroes. They speak about their careers to date and offer some insights on what it takes to lead and to nurture successful organisations. Not everyone we approached agreed to be involved – many inspirational leaders are missing – and a phalanx of in-house PR people threw as many obstacles as possible to thwart us in our attempts to get anywhere near some! Some of the people we approached seemed to live in fear of what their Non-Execs or major shareholders would think. Of course, we were never looking to trip anyone up. We were simply hoping to gain some of their insights, hear about their business remedies and catch glimpses of their wisdom. We are deeply indebted to those who did agree to be interviewed. We are delighted to have compiled a fabulous selection of some extraordinary leaders.

We've divided the interviews into four sections. These follow a broadly chronological order, but more to the point, reflect the underlying global economic and social context, and the different stages of development of Q5 as a business.

Before we dive in, a note on the title: Magic Sponge – for those with an interest in British sport in the 70s and 80s the term 'magic sponge' needs no explanation. For those that don't… a magic sponge is a sponge much like any other sponge, except when it is wielded by football or rugby physio running on to the pitch to attend to an injured player. When this happens, the sponge is transformed into a universal panacea so that it can heal anything from a bruised shin to a broken collar bone.

Organisation physiotherapy was a concept we at Q5 explored from the outset, the idea that organisational fitness was neither a natural state nor one easy to achieve. When we started Q5 in 2009 many businesses had already cut their workforce once, twice, even three times. In many cases they not only had trimmed the 'fat' but had cut deep into the muscle of the organisation. Many of our first projects were not only about cutting costs (the surgery), but also about making what was left fit for purpose (the physio). When we began interviewing some of our clients for our newsletters, 'the magic sponge' just seemed to fit.

We hope you enjoy it.

‘Look how this ha’ growen an’ growen sir, bigger an’ bigger,
broader an’ broader, harder an’ harder,
fro year to year, fro generation unto generation.
Who can look on’t sir, and fairly tell a man ‘tis not a muddle?’

— Charles Dickens, *Hard Times*

Lord Stevenson of Coddenham, CBE, DL
Mike Clasper, CBE
Dame Carolyn McCall, DBE
Nigel Railton
Sharon Rice-Oxley

QUARTER ONE

2010–2012 Hard Times

2007-2011

ON THE PLUS SIDE OF ALL THIS, AT LEAST WE ARE NO LONGER THE MOST HATED PROFESSION IN THE COUNTRY!
FOR SALE
BANK
P45
STUFF
ESTATE AGENTS

Q5 ventured unsteadily into the world in April 2009, in the midst of the Global Financial Crisis. Not a great time to start a business, many people told us. There were moments early on when we considered they might have a point, but we had faith in what we were doing, and much of the work we did in those early years was related to the belt-tightening that characterised much of the late 00's and early 10's

In this section we speak to Dennis Stevenson, friend of Q5, and holder of numerous board and public positions including Chairman of HBOS, Pearson, and Aldeburgh Music, and Chancellor of University of Arts London. Dennis reflects on many aspects of his life and career with his inimitable clear-sighted and left-field thinking. Mike Clasper, then Chairman of HM Revenue & Customs, talks about his experience across the public and private sectors, and offers some insight on how to drive business performance when times are hard.

Carolyn McCall shares the joys and challenges of moving from the privately-owned Guardian Media Group to the very public easyJet, and amidst the austerity Nigel Railton tells us how Camelot shared the wealth. We close this section with Sharon Rice-Oxley, whose journey to co-founding Q5 included stops in Perestroika Russia, big consulting, infrastructure and self-employment.

Nerves are a good thing.

Baron Stevenson of Coddenham, CBE, DL

POSITION AT TIME OF INTERVIEW:
Serial and Social Entrepreneur & Retired FTSE100 Chairman (UK-based)

Born and raised in Scotland, Dennis Stevenson had originally planned for an entirely "anti-business" career in academia, but through his 'greatest escape' (and one sub-optimal exam result!) he has ended up spending his entire career in prominent leadership roles across the business world, investing in somewhere between 70- 100 start ups and spending roughly half his time on social causes.

Throughout the '90s and '00s Dennis was the Chair of several FTSE100 companies, including HBOS during the financial crisis, and was the Chairman of the Trustees of the Tate Gallery that built Tate Modern.

More recently, Dennis has been a leading campaigner and government advisor on mental health, having set up the world's leading mental health research foundation, and has talked publicly and inspirationally about his own battles with mental health throughout his career.

Where did you grow up?

I was born in Edinburgh. I lived there or thereabouts until I was 17, so I consider Edinburgh to be my roots. I still have a flat there. My wife is much less keen on Edinburgh than I am, but I'm allowed to go there from time to time!

When did you meet Charlotte, your wife, and how would she describe you?

I met Charlotte at the end of my first year at Cambridge. We didn't get married for seven years, and we were "divorced" at least three times before we even got married! But, for me, it was love at first sight. Charlotte would describe me as 'impossible'. We've got four children, but Charlotte would say she has five! She said she married me for two reasons: one was that she knew she'd never be bored and second, she had spotted that I was very paternal. She didn't think she would be very maternal. As it turns out, she is.

When did you discover your passion for business?

I was, and still am, left-wing and, in some sense, rather anti-business. My problem was my final exams at Cambridge. I had planned to be an academic and to go to America for research. My college (Kings) wanted to put me up for a Harkness Fellowship. But I got a bad degree (2:2). I left university without a job to go to. The brother-in-law of a friend started a business, and I became his first employee. He was great but completely hopeless at managing. So, at the age of 22 I became the MD of a fast-expanding business. It turned out that I was quite good at managing the business; I like changing things and making things happen. So, what seemed the greatest disaster of all time – missing out on a career in academia – was the greatest escape I'd ever had. I'm now in the process of investing in something like my 100th start up.

What is it in number 100 that you're looking for?

I am completely people driven. Of course, you have to have some sense that the business is a good idea. But my main thing is the people. Do I like and trust them? Do I rate them? I am meticulous about that. I have found that this is far more important than anything else.

What will be your advice to your grandchildren, when they complete their education? Would you encourage them to start a business at that point?

In my generation, you tended to work in a "conventional" business setting until you were in your early 30s. I think that's silly, because in your early 30s you've got a mortgage, possibly children so I am a great believer in starting early. This leads to a related thought. Nowadays there's an unholy alliance between the venture capital industry and business schools. This encourages dysfunctional behaviour; people produce business plans, spreadsheets and DCFs which tend to encourage ridiculously ambitious ideas and processes. Actually, many successful entrepreneurs start in a shed; one step forward, one step back, three steps forward and a big knock – four steps back. It may not work the first time. But there's more chance it will the second time. My advice is start young. Don't be too pretentious. Do it gradually.

But I would not assume that my grandchildren should go into business. I would encourage them to think of the huge satisfaction they could get out of working in not for profit activities and improving the lives of their fellow human beings.

Many young business-people that we work with talk about controlling personal fears and nerves. Do you get nervous? If so, how do you manage that?
Nerves are a good thing. It's said that the great Donald Bradman was always nervous when he went out to bat, even though he was the greatest cricketer that's ever lived. Nerves are good because they sharpen you. A nerveless person isn't a real human. There's no substitute for putting the work into something, getting it sorted and knowing that you've got every base covered. I have sometimes given the impression that I'm winging it. But, I've hardly ever winged anything in my life. I've got to meet my grandchildren's piano teacher tomorrow afternoon. I'm already nervous about it and there will be several other occasions this week when I'll be nervous.

Yet you establish a presence in a room very easily. How do you do this?
It's just how I am. It's not a deliberate thing! I like talking! I'm sure it is something you can develop, but you do have to play to your strengths. I have one or two friends who are rather quiet men or women. But they can create a big impact too. There's no disguising the fact that I'm noisy! I was about 40 when someone explained the effect that I had on a room. I'm very grateful that I do have some sort of effect! It has stood me in good stead most of the time.

A lot of leadership and management books talk about 'authentic leadership'. Are you the same Dennis that is known to your family as you are to any other group that you interact with?
I hope so. Authentic leadership is good. Many of the leaders that I've met in my life have been rather sad people without proper human relations with their family or their friends. Some of them are more stuck on appearances. I hope it's improving.

Who do you admire as a leader?
Without doubt, Mandela is the greatest leader in my lifetime. He was good in all weathers regardless of what was happening. He was certainly a leader of men and women; the kind of person whom you would

follow over the barricades. He was brilliant. I regret to say that I find it difficult to identify more than a handful of people at the top of quoted companies that I really admire. The leaders I admire are the people who haven't buckled in the face of pressure. They are people who have been consistent. It's easier said than done. It is quite easy to look good when you are successful. It is less easy to be consistent when you are not.

What did you learn from your own experiences as chairman of the HBOS board in the late '00s?
Not a great deal. All of us failed to forecast the collapse of wholesale markets. HBOS actually did more than most other banks to anticipate it. One of the things I *have* learnt is that economic forecasting doesn't work. During my lifetime no one's got forecasting consistently right. So, in all my businesses, I say to them, "Know that, at any point in time, you have to be able to survive a disaster."

When was the first time you talked about mental health openly?
Oh, about 30 years ago. By the time I realised I had mental health issues I was successful, not exactly poor, had a wife and children who seemed to enjoy me being around and a lot of friends so I reckoned if I didn't talk about it who would? I became involved in mental health of course as a result of my own experiences. I helped set up the world's leading mental health foundation. I put through the key legislation in this country and I wrote a report on mental health at work (Thriving at Work, 2017). This report has been adopted in the UK Public Sector. I will be surprised and disappointed if, two years from now, every single one of the top 250 companies in the UK hasn't changed how it deals with mental health.

The real challenge is how to get that down to the Smaller to Medium Sized businesses. The biggest challenge of all is how to effect this change in the gig economy. I recognise that there are limits to what else I can do. However, I'm optimistic. It's not difficult to see what needs to happen. If you ask someone on the street how their mental health is, they'll think you're talking about an illness. We've got to move from a society that is like that, to one where people realise that everyone has 'mental health'. Just like our physical health, we must learn how to manage our mental health, and be more aware of other people's. We need to bring our children up to realise that they have both physical and mental health.

Do you have a mantra for life?
Not really. I've got fairly strong moral principles, which is very easy for me to have because I don't have too many moral dilemmas. I think, "Count your blessings!" is probably the nearest to a mantra. I'm very intolerant of people who behave badly, of whom sadly there are lots.

Who has been the biggest influence on your professional life?
A guy called David Astor was very important. He inherited The *Observer* and was the great left-of-centre, liberal editor of his generation. I was very lucky David became my mentor. He was quite rich, but he gave his money away very thoughtfully and very cleverly. I have wanted and tried to do the same. I have been increasingly incensed by the inequality in the world. I became Chairman of the development organisation, ITDG (Intermediate Technology Development Group). It was effectively bust when I joined it and that's why I was brought in. We concluded that the only way the business could raise money was through direct marketing. The problem was we needed a nest egg to finance a direct marketing campaign. I was pretty desperate when David came to lunch and put an envelope in my hand. He said, 'This is for you to invest in your direct marketing'. The envelope had a cheque for £250k in it! I am proud to say we used it to create a substantial regular income which put the organisation on a sustainable path. When Charlotte and I sat down, aged 40, and thought about what we wanted to do with the rest of our lives, we asked ourselves who we most admired. We thought of David.

What is your greatest achievement?
It may sound corny but my marriage and family are my greatest achievements. It is built on trust. My children all want to talk to me. They're each other's best friends. Aside from my family life the Thriving at Work report that Paul Farmer and I wrote for the Prime Minister in 2017 is my greatest achievement. It is probably going to influence the lives of tens of millions of people. It's already influencing the lives of many. The UK health service is changing as a result of it. If I'm still alive in 10 years' time, I'm hopeful that our nation will realise that 'mental health' is not an illness.

Interview: JG, London

Be curious and be approachable.

Mike Clasper, CBE

POSITION AT TIME OF INTERVIEW:
Chairman of Her Majesty's Revenue & Customs, Government (UK-based)

Mike Clasper was one of the first 'Magic Sponges' that we ever conducted, in 2010. At the time, Mike was the non-executive Chairman of HM Revenue and Customs, a board member of ITV plc, and Chairman of the commercial branch of Which... And frankly we felt bloody lucky as a small consultancy upstart that he was willing to give up his time for us (and he has remained a firm friend of Q5 ever since)!

Mike has been awarded a CBE, as well as an honorary doctorate from Sunderland University. He is a Sunderland FC fan, which means he has been able to develop quite a thick skin over the years!

Mike worked for Proctor & Gamble for 23 years and, at the turn of the millennium was the CEO of British Airport Authority (BAA). In recent years, Mike has served as president of the Chartered Management Institute and is currently Chairman of Coats Group plc.

Given the financial climate at the time of our interview, and his deep experience of both the public and private sectors, we wanted to ask Mike about running different types of businesses at a time of austerity - and the challenges this presented.

What should business leaders do to drive performance in this economy?
The financial situation that we find ourselves in is, unquestionably, one of high stress. To some extent, the bland answer to this question is: 'Do everything better'. However, I think there are a couple of areas that business leaders need to focus on.

First, many businesses are cash strapped. A relentless focus on managing cash, not profit, will put your business in a strong position for recovery.

Second, many customer segments are feeling the pain too. With the Government focusing on closing the deficit, consumers are feeling uncertain about the future. There are low returns on savings, tax increases, shorter working weeks, which means that they won't spend as much. Business leaders, therefore, have to redouble their efforts for the customer segments that are most important to them. They need to focus on what their customers value, particularly in these tougher times, and generate even more value for them without adding cost.

What key business developments do you see in the year ahead?
It is unlikely that we are going to bounce back quickly, this is not a 'V' valley dip with a quick, sharp recovery. I foresee three developments:

Consolidation – well-known brand names, like Woolworths, have already disappeared and others will go the same way. Companies are struggling for market-share, particularly in sectors that are highly fragmented, so we will see more takeovers. Leaders will look for ways to add value through consolidation, driving out efficiencies and gaining as much market-share as possible.

Entrepreneurialism – there are many supremely talented people losing their jobs. There will be a natural tendency for entrepreneurship at a micro-level, with people using their severance packages to set up new business – either on their own or joining up with others.

Exports will hopefully increase – we have weak sterling. Our large fiscal deficit means lower exchange rates for the foreseeable future, which is a good thing for businesses that export their goods abroad.

Having worked in both sectors, what are the best things that you would take from the public sector and private sector to make a truly fabulous business?
The public sector has a very strong sense of purpose. People want to do the right thing, whether that is enabling children to gain better education or helping people to recover from illness and injury. Given the size, scale and complexity of public sector organisations, there are so many issues

that could crop up that simply don't due to the moral judgment of the people who work in them.

On the other hand, the private sector has a much stronger customer focus. They are demand-led so organisations must be adept at looking through the eyes of their customers and delivering the services and products customers want. This is an ethos that private sector leaders instil in the minds of all their employees, and public sector organisations lag well behind. Financial disciplines are also more rigorous in the private sector, with a focus on cost and value-for-money that is rarely matched in the public sector.

Business leaders in the private sector are highly skilled at using strategy to drive resource prioritisation. The next Government, whoever it is, will have to make very tough choices. Public sector leaders have been operating in a 'field of plenty' but will now have to make significant savings for several years. They will need to show the same ability; using strategy to determine resource allocation, which private sector leaders do year in, year out.

Who has inspired you most in your career?
My father ran a small contract building business. He developed strong, lasting working relationships with everyone connected to his business, from the carpenters to builders in the business, to the contracted plumbers and electricians. He made himself accessible to all and instilled in me a belief that it is the men and women working on the front-line who really count. I have been fortunate enough to work with many great people throughout my career, leaders who have shaped my views and influenced me in many ways, but it is my father who has inspired me the most.

What is your own personal business motto?
'Be curious and be approachable.' This was my father's motto, but I have claimed it as my own!

Interview: OP, London

If you end up 'doing change' to people, the process is doomed.

Dame Carolyn McCall, DBE

POSITION AT TIME OF INTERVIEW:
CEO of Easyjet, Aviation (UK-based)

Born in Bangalore, educated in India and Singapore, Carolyn's early life would be worthy of an interview on its own. However, Carolyn is one of the busiest CEOs around, and we had a limited amount of time with her.

So, we focused on her business career. We interviewed Carolyn in May 2011, shortly after she had taken the reins at EasyJet.

Prior to this appointment, Carolyn was the Chief Executive of Guardian Media Group, and held Non-Executive directorships at Tesco and New Look. Through our interview, we wanted to find out about making the leap from running a private company to running a publicly listed company – and indeed going from owning the news agenda to potentially being the news agenda!

Since the time of our interview, Carolyn has since been the non-Executive Director of Lloyds TSB, the first ever female Chief Executive of ITV, and a non-executive board member of the Department for BEIS and was awarded a Damehood in 2016.

Carolyn, easyJet delivers a value-for-money 'no frills' service. How do you engage your people not to fall into the trap of providing a 'cheap' customer experience?
It depends which part of the customer experience you are dealing with. We have complete control of the onboard experience; the cabin crew are easyJet employees. We recruit, train, manage and incentivise them. And they're fantastic. There is a real camaraderie among them. They love the brand and they really enjoy their jobs. I get emails all the time from passengers praising their onboard experience, which is all down to our hard-working crews.

We have mapped every single point in the process where our product comes into contact with the customer. Our focus on the passenger is what truly differentiates us. It is where we build brand affinity, and where we generate loyalty.

Yet there are certain parts of the customer experience where we must cede direct control of the process to others; for instance, airport staff. We use our leverage and influence with airports, ground handlers and other external stakeholders to encourage them to be friendly and helpful to our customers. It is not an economic issue; it costs nothing to be friendly. It's about caring, smiling, being welcoming and wanting to serve each passenger in the right way. So externally we influence our partners where we can, and internally, we hire the right people and make sure we develop them.

How do you reflect your internal brand in your external brand? What do you have to do to line the two things up?
The employer brand and the external brand must be one and the same. I carried out a brand audit as soon as I arrived at easyJet to make sure there were no gaps between what we say the brand is and the actual experience our customers have with us. If you say your brand is one of integrity, openness and helpfulness… you clearly must be so.

Another early priority was to appoint a marketing director with deep expertise in customer insight AND a strong understanding of brand building. Both attributes are required for driving behaviours internally and externally. You want your people to live and breathe your brand and become very strong advocates of it.

In recent years easyJets' brand positioning has focused on price, but there are many other important elements to easyJet. We beat Ryanair hands down on customer experience, but the real win for us is to demonstrate that we're better at short haul than the Bas and Air Frances. easyJet must stand for convenience, good value, and being acutely passenger focused.

How important do you see employee engagement during a change process?
It is the single most important thing. Statistically 80% of change programmes fail. When change is imposed on people it fails to achieve 'buy in'. If people don't feel the need for change, they block it. Of course, change must be led by the top team; but leaders have to engage people at all levels. They must listen to their thoughts, encourage new ideas and get them actively involved in the process. If you end up 'doing change' to people, the process is doomed.

Do you think that male and female leaders approach employee engagement differently?
I don't think it is gender specific. It really depends on one's personality; some people do it quietly and confidently, some are more extrovert and exuberant. Some don't do it at all.

How have you found the experience of moving from a privately-owned organisation to a nakedly commercial one where there is constant pressure to manage the margins and satisfy shareholders?
The biggest difference is the relentlessness of quarterly reporting. You feel like you are constantly on the road talking to investors and analysts. The speed at which the quarterly reports come upon you … it can really feel like minutes! The other difference is the short-term nature of quarterly reporting; you might approach half-year with one set of figures, whilst you know that Q3 is going to be stellar. There is a rhythm and a ritual that you must get used to which is quite different from working in a privately-owned business.

And finally, who has been the biggest influence on your career?
There are many. The Guardian opened me up to some fantastic people; Alan Rusbridger and Caroline Marland have been very big influences on me. I learnt how to manage people at the Guardian, how to really get the best out of them in a very creative and challenging environment. People underestimate how tough the Guardian is; it was a real meritocracy. My experience at Tesco has also influenced me enormously. Working on the Board with people like Mervyn Davies, Charles Allen, Karen Cook, David Reid – an amazing array of non-execs – not to mention Sir Terry Leahy and a formidable executive team, taught me a great deal about how PLCs operate.

Interview: OP, London

The thing I look for is empathy. If you have a team of empathetic people, you are going to be successful.

Nigel Railton

POSITION AT TIME OF INTERVIEW:
CEO of Camelot, National Lottery (UK-based)

Nigel Railton is the CEO of Camelot UK Lotteries and Camelot Global. He was born in Crewe, and came from humble, but happy origins.

We were initially keen to find out about the organisation and its distribution of wealth at a time of extreme financial difficulty. But it soon became clear that Nigel had an extraordinary personal career tale to tell: There are few people around who can claim to have started work in the rail industry as a signal box lad, owned and run a hair salon and a pub, become a qualified accountant and eventually ended up as the CEO of the UK's largest lottery group – whose UK sales last year were bigger than the combined UK sales of Cadbury, Coca-Cola, Nestle, Walkers, Heinz, Warburtons and Purina.
But that is exactly what Nigel has done.

So alongside the challenges at Camelot, the interview explores Nigel's broader career – not going to university, getting (nearly) "fired" from his first job, and experiencing one lottery winner's unusual crumpet-based celebration!

Did you always want to get into business?
When I was younger, I wanted to be a vet. Coming from Crewe, in Cheshire, there are not a lot of opportunities for vets, so I found myself working on the railways at 16 as a signal box lad. Living in Crewe in the early '80s, there were only three choices when you left school; work on the railway, work for Rolls-Royce, or go on the dole. Many of my friends chose the third option. I didn't really have any goals at that point. I knew I wanted to be successful, but I didn't know how.

You went straight from school into work at 16. Did you ever think about university?
It was never really an option in my family. No-one had ever been to university or been professionally qualified. In Crewe, you followed the route of your parents. If your parents worked on the railway then that is what you did. When I was 18, I realised that this was not what I wanted to do. I was always very bright at school, but my parents didn't really have many aspirations for me; what success looked like to them was just having a steady job. At 18, I moved to working in the booking office, selling tickets. I decided at that point that I wanted to study for accountancy qualifications.

The booking office was pseudo-financial and gave me the option to start studying. I did a lot of study-at-night classes and at weekends. I got a job in regional finance for British Rail in Birmingham. I travelled there for three years - an hour each way on the train. People in Crewe never did that; they thought I was mad. By 21, I was the youngest ever management grade on the railway.

Given that approach, what do you think about the fact that there is more encouragement for people to seek other ways of progression, like apprenticeship schemes, rather than going to university?
It's all about balance. The same thing doesn't work for everybody. But, at Camelot, we're going to look at apprenticeships as a key part of our future. Apprentices can provide a different insight into things. People get a different outlook on life, depending on the route they take. I am going to encourage my kids to go to university … if they want to.

Why do you want to encourage them to go to university?
I like to give them the opportunities that I never had. When I was a kid, my dad came home from work and put his pay packet into a box in the living room – that was the extent of the money we had. And I thought, 'I want more than this.'

Do you think businesses could do more to look for talent outside of traditional sources?

You often don't get opportunities unless you tick all the boxes. Sometimes you must look beyond the boxes and see the people.

When did your plan to meet your end-goal fall into place?

I was always an entrepreneur and wanted to own a business. I had a hairdressing business at 21 and a pub at 25. Not that I was a hairdresser, but my ex-girlfriend was. I made some money in the property boom in Crewe in '88 and invested in a business that she's still got today. However, I thought the best route to get into any senior position was via accountancy. So, I moved to Watford in '92 to go to accountancy tutors in London. I qualified in '95 and my career really took off.

Was there any point in your journey that nearly pushed you off plan?

I tell my son this story about resilience and never giving up…I got this job in Watford as a relatively senior accountant but didn't have the experience to do it well. I remember waking up one morning in a bedsit, in a new town, with a new job. I decided there were two ways I could fix this; I could give up or I could work even harder. I asked someone in the office to help me – which is a lesson in life to never be afraid to ask for assistance from people – and I worked long hours every night for about a month. After that, it all seemed to click into place.

Do you think your upbringing has shaped the way you work?

I've always been driven but I'm also a great believer in empathy as an important management tool. I treat everyone the same. I never speak to anyone differently, from the people cleaning the toilets to our new Chairman, Hugh Robertson. Has my background influenced me? Probably. Some of the feedback I get is that I am approachable, consistent and normal.

Do you think there's a good fit between your background and the beneficiaries of National Lottery money, in terms of how you interact?

About a year ago, I went to a council estate in Glasgow. The big lottery fund had funded a community allotment centre. People grow food on derelict land that has been converted into allotments to try to change the diets of the local children and society in general. All the people working there are volunteers. I saw what a difference the lottery was making. Because I was born on a council estate, I could resonate with it immediately. It gave me a real sense of drive and purpose.

Given the challenges reported in the press for Camelot around how much money goes to good causes, what do you think are the ingredients that will change perceptions?
The National Lottery is a system. Camelot are only the operators of the games, the channels and the marketing. The other side is about good causes, distribution and award of grants – and we don't control that. When people have a bad experience getting grants it can have a bearing on their relationship with the National Lottery. We are now working very closely with the National Lottery community fund to make sure that we work together. We are doing that through relationships rather than any legal framework. A year ago, there was no relationship at all and now we are designing a joint operating model together.

When you see people from less advantaged backgrounds buying tickets, do you see that as an appropriate connection?
The National Lottery is for everybody. Our problem is not the people from a more disadvantaged background – it's the people who are classed as middle class and upwards who don't play. We need to attract more ABC1s to play the National Lottery. They play the big jackpots but not as habitually as we would like. The trick is to get a portfolio of games that appeals to everybody. You have to give people a game they want to play and make it exciting. You must remind them why they want to play.

Is the connection between playing and outcome – not just on them as individuals but on society – something you want to emphasise?
People don't play the National Lottery to give to good causes, otherwise they would give directly to charity. What's important is that if people don't win, they feel good about playing because they have made a difference. We need to work with the distribution bodies to link winners to locations, and the timelier it is the larger the impact it has. I was in Northern Ireland, in Belfast, which has these beautiful gardens that have been funded by the National Lottery and they cost about £3 million. I went to a little retailer in the city centre that had raised £2 million. I asked them whether they realised they had done this – raised two-thirds of the money. Once you start making that connection, it is amazing.

Do you have a special winner's story that resonates with you?
I was privileged enough to go to a winners' event in York. It took my life full circle. It was my first engagement as permanent CEO, and I was only there by pure coincidence. I was standing in the National Rail Museum surrounded by big locos that my grandad used to drive, addressing 250 millionaires. It was surreal. I met Andy, from Hull, who told me that his wife had called him and said they had won a million. They had previously been on Weight Watchers and he said, 'sod Weight Watchers, we are millionaires.' He went out a bought a packet of crumpets and a tub of *Lurpak* and ate the lot. I asked him what difference it made to him, and

he said, 'my boiler's just broken down and I don't have to worry about where the money comes from to fix it.' We have made over 5,000 people millionaires since the National Lottery was launched, generating £39 billion for good causes and transforming the UK.

What is it that gets you out of bed in the morning?
It is realising the responsibility that I and the organisation have to keep raising money for good causes. I was talking to a woman from Liverpool who runs a charity supermarket funded by the National Lottery. She was telling me about this guy who came in for food with his two-year-old child who hadn't eaten for three days. He was self-employed and his van had broken down. He couldn't afford to get it fixed so he couldn't work and therefore he had no money. If it wasn't for the work that we do, in terms of providing those facilities, he would not be able to go there for food. If we don't perform as Camelot, lots of people suffer.

If you could give your 20-year-old self some advice, what would you say?
Slow down a bit. When you are in your 20s and 30s, there is a drive and urgency to get somewhere. As you get older, you realise that life is a marathon, not a sprint. You are going to get there anyway so you might as well slow down and enjoy the ride.

What do you see as being the real key to your success?
Never giving up. There is always a way, you just have to find it.

What happens when you work with people who are driven in another way?
You need balance and commonality. The thing I look for is empathy. If you have a team of empathetic people, you are going to be successful. People will be thinking about each other, not just themselves. I also think you have got to be consistent as a leader. People need to know that when I turn up to work, they are going to meet the same person every day.

Is there a mentor from whom you have learnt a lot?
Back when I was a signal box lad, I will never forget Larry Eidelman. I fell asleep during the night when I should have been doing my job. He woke me up and told me I was fired. He let me get to the door before telling me he had covered my job and said, 'don't do that again, son'. It taught me about treating people right and the impact you can have on people. George Woodall, my boss in Birmingham, taught me to treat everyone fairly. He was very flexible with people and would give us time off. For the last 30 years, if people wanted the afternoon off, I would tell them not to take it as holiday and have the afternoon off. In return, when we are busy, I expected them to put in a shift. People really liked it, as I was putting trust in them. Without exception over the years, that has always worked for me.

People see you as a leader. What makes you good in your role?
I have been in quite a senior position for a long time. I have had the privilege of working for good leaders and learning from them. And I am still learning today. I mean, our Chairman, Hugh Robertson, is an amazing guy. But what has made me a good leader is experience – making mistakes but learning from them.

If you were starting out today, what would you say about how to view your career?
Don't expect too much. Think about what you can give rather than receive. I think there is a bit more of an expectation now that you are going to get rather than give.

What about the split between work and home life? Do you take your problems home?
I try not to but sometimes that is easier said than done. It is important that my family see me, not the CEO. I also make sure I have holidays as often as I can with the kids; I remind them we are lucky to be able to do this because of what I do but it is where we can be truly 'us'.

What are your hopes for the business?
We hope to be around for a long time in the UK National Lottery and plan to get it into good health. We recently did a strategic review and identified lots of things we need to fix. We have a plan, which we've implemented, and it is working. We are hoping to generate even more for the National Lottery over the next two years than we are doing already.

And when you eventually stop working, how do you want people to remember you?
That 'he was alright.' That would be good.

Interview: CP, London

Don't expect too much. Think about what you can give rather than receive.

I think the best leaders are the people that give freedom.

Sharon Rice-Oxley

POSITION AT TIME OF INTERVIEW:
Partner, Q5. Consulting Sector (Global)

Sharon is one of the co-founders of Q5.

She has been described as "one of the most sought-after business advisors of her generation," admittedly by Sharon herself, who seemed surprisingly keen to help edit her own introduction.

Born in Northampton, Sharon fell in love with Russia in her teenage years and lived there for a few years before starting her consulting career in London.

Since then, Sharon has amassed a quarter of a century's experience working in the consulting sector, specialising in organisation design and change management. She is unnervingly straight to the point and intolerant of all waffle (not something all consultants are universally famous for). She's the mother of three teenagers, a Trustee at the mental health charity, and enjoys playing hockey when she can.

In this interview, we grill Sharon about her unconventional career moves – from her dream to be a James Bond-esque spy (entirely unclear whether achieved or not) through to setting up Q5 at the height of the financial crisis with a group of people she knew next to nothing about.

Going back to your teenage years, what did you study at university?
I studied at Exeter University, and I did a joint honours degree in Russian and German. I was a languages student.

Did you show any early signs of 'business nous' when you were a student?
No, none whatsoever – it was all about languages for me. I chose Russian at University because I wanted to be a spy! It was the end of the Cold War, when I was at school, and there were lots of James Bond movies involving Soviet spies. I thought, "Yeah, I can go behind the iron curtain!" – of course, the iron curtain still existed when I started learning Russian. So, I went to Exeter, learnt Russian from scratch – which was phenomenally hard work, but brilliant – and then went to Russia as a student. This was just the most exhilarating experience; the culture, the language, the people – I fell in love with the place.

How long did you spend in Russia?
On and off, about 10 years; pretty much up until I had kids.

Did you deliver on your spying aspirations?
I'd have to shoot you if I told you! I graduated in 1992, during a recession. All my friends were desperately trying to get jobs on the 'milk round' but they couldn't, as there were so few jobs around. So, I thought, 'I'll go to Russia – why would I waste these four years of study?' Whilst I was there, I saw Russia go through Perestroika and Glasnost.

So, you were pretty green when you jetted off to Moscow then. How did things turn out?
Yes, I was 21 – my father cried when I left; one of the few times I've seen him cry. As I reached the plane, he asked whether he would ever see me again!

When I arrived, I went to the British Embassy and asked for a list of all the British companies based in Moscow. Back then, there were about 150 British companies there. I wrote to all of them saying, 'Please can I have a job. I can speak Russian.' Amazingly, quite a few got back to me. This was because the country was beginning to open up, and it was quite rare, back then, for a young British woman arriving in Moscow able to speak Russian. For me, there was an early realisation that you didn't have to go through working life via 'the normal route'. You didn't have to follow the crowd. If you tried and were able to push the boundary just a little bit, people often say 'okay, we'll give it a shot.'

What was your first actual job in Russia?
My first Russian job was in sales and marketing for a small British company that sold EPOS systems (electronic point of sales). I worked for a woman who had been in the army, before becoming an entrepreneur. She had managed to secure the EPOS licence and then sold it across Russia. I basically went out and did sales and marketing for her. I hated it! That said, it was a good lesson in how to win business, and I admired her greatly. She was very charismatic and had utter belief in herself. The funny thing was, she didn't pay me a salary when I first got there. She told me that she would cover my weekly food bill, and that I could go and spend whatever I wanted in this supermarket. That's basically how I got paid for the first three months. I then cottoned on, and was like, "Hang on a minute, I want some money!"

So, after a while, I imagine you looked for another job?
Yes, I had three jobs in Russia. In that first stint, I did sales and marketing, then I moved to Ernst & Young, before finally working for the European Commission in HR. At that point I realised there was this thing called 'business' and I needed to get better qualified. I came back to the UK and did an MBA. That's how I found consulting. At the back end of that, I joined Andersen Consulting (now known as Accenture).

Consulting was still a relatively new thing in the early '90s. What were your early influences in consulting? Did you have any role models when you first started?
Accenture was a great place to learn the consulting trade. I think probably my biggest role models were the team-mates around me, because people were from different walks of life and had different experiences.

As I got further into my Accenture career, there became clearer role models. One of those, who I would count as a good friend now, is John Downie. I worked with John when I got back from Russia in 1999, on the BP account. He was an Associate Partner at that stage. The way he put a team together – and the freedom he gave people – was wonderful. I think the best leaders are the people that give freedom.

In your early years of Accenture, did you focus on one industry sector or did you roam across industry sectors?
When I joined, they didn't have a sector-focus. I was very much in the 'change management' space. When the firm moved to having a sector-focus, I was initially put in Financial Services. However, I moved to Russia in 1998 and went into Resources. I pretty much stayed there – working primarily on the BP account – until I left Accenture in 2003.

In your early years at Accenture you worked in change. You're best known for being a bit of a guru in the world of Organisation Design. When did you first get into the world of org design?

I think it was always something that I was reaching for in Accenture. I can't quite remember but in my early years of consulting I started out doing training, learning & development and communications. I realised after a while that there was a bridge between Strategy and Change, which was something called 'Organisation Design'.

Did you 'learn on the job' when you first started out practising Organisation Design?

It was all on the job for me. The big shift was when I left Accenture and went to head up Organisation Design & Development at the British Airports Authority (BAA). That was where I really honed my skills because I was doing organisation design and development with an executive team who really believed in it. We were shaping the whole organisation and doing design and development from all angles.

Fast forward 10 years and you've maintained strong relationships with so many of your colleagues from that era. What was it about that particular team at BAA?

I think it was largely down to the CEO, Mike Clasper (who is interviewed elsewhere in this book). He had a real vision for BAA. It was an organisation that had been through privatisation, but it had failed to become customer-focused and truly change itself. What he allowed his executive team to do was to build an internal capability. So I joined the Organisation Design & Development group. The thinking was to not bring in consultants to do it, but to have a group of well-trained internal consultants that could commit to the BAA journey instead. Because of that, we brought in a lot of talented people over that period – and they have gone on to do lots of different and interesting things.

After BAA, you worked as a 'sole trader' for a period of a time. Did you enjoy that?

Yes, I had another child. By that time, I had three small children under the age of five. BAA was taken over while I was on maternity leave, and I decided to leave and do my own thing for a while, as I needed some flexibility. This was quite a big step, because I'd been employed since I left university. There was that moment of, 'I'm going to try this. How's it going to go?' I picked up the phone to John Downie at Accenture and told him what I was going to do, and he immediately said, 'Come in and help us!' That first moment, where I was selling myself as an individual on-the-market, was a big moment. I believed in myself. I guess I had sort of done that at the beginning of my career; I had come full circle in a way.

At the same time, you set up a company called 'Professional Parents'.
I had an absolute ball for the first year, freelancing two days a week – pretty much all with Accenture, but with a few other bits and pieces thrown in. But I very quickly started reaching for the next thing and I realised that what I was doing wasn't enough for me. It was good, and it was flexible for the family, but I personally wanted something different. As a lot of people do when they go through a family transition, I started looking at what it means for couples and what they need to do to set themselves up for success. I set up a small coaching outfit called 'Professional Parents'. I did a lot of research, had lots of interviews, created templates and coaching paths for couples to join, and started building a little roster of coaches to work with.

The story of Q5 is known to some people who will be reading this book, but I am interested to find out what the most nerve-wracking thing was for you about setting up the business?
The most nerve-wracking thing was that I didn't know everybody. I knew you (Olly Purnell) and Carla (Schaeffer) a little, but there was a real leap of faith that I could do it with this group of people. However, the team thing turned out to be great. That said, it was probably what I had most sleepless nights over. Also, at that time of life, with small kids, there was something significant in the fact that I was stepping back into something that I could really commit to.

All your work is focused on client projects, working with clients on a day to day basis, keeping in touch with clients. What's your definition of the perfect client?
For me, the perfect client is somebody that wants to be in partnership. They want it to be a long-term stakeholder. They trust us to be there in their time of need. They know that they can pick up the phone and we will mobilise quickly in the best possible way, with an excellent team. They know that we are doing it for all the right reasons – for positive intent. That comes from depth of personal relationship. It's a personal thing for me. It might not be the same for everybody. Those clients, with whom I've been able to build that depth of a relationship, are the most rewarding by some distance.

There will be some clients who have known you for 25 years or so. How have you adapted and evolved your role over that period?
I think of my role at Q5 in phases. In the first year it was all about introducing people that knew me ... to this 'thing' that I was part of. I was always very involved in those early three or four years, very hands-on and, as we were able to build our team, I was able to take a step back. All the clients that I've worked with in those 25 years, they know that if they

need me, they can always pick up the phone and I will answer, but I also trust our team to do the work that they need to do.

Keeping clients engaged and keeping relationships strong has always been the secret sauce for you.
Actually, I think the secret sauce is curiosity. I think it is curiosity – 'what would happen if we did something, what would be the outcome if we made this or that change for the organisation and for the individual' and caring enough to then see it through. As soon as a consultant is mechanistic in running a project and isn't connected to the individual, that's when they are not asked back. I think that's why Q5 gets asked back time and again – because we are inherently and consistently curious about what's going on for our clients.

What advice would you give to someone at the very beginning of their career?
I genuinely think you must follow your heart's desire in terms of the subject you want to study. Find your passion. Build on it. Ultimately *this* is what will take you places. I'd really encourage people not to worry about what they are going to be. Instead, they should take every opportunity for what it is, get the most out of it and use it as a stepping-stone to the next thing.

Looking ahead to the day when you eventually leave Q5, what would you like to think and feel about the experience?
I'd like to feel that there's a team of people that can take it on beyond me – that there's long-term sustainability. It probably won't look exactly as it's looked to date, but it will exist and go on to be something different. Hopefully, something even better!

Interview: OP, London

THIS IS WHAT I HAVE BEEN WORKING ON FOR SO LONG GUYS...... ....I AM GOING TO CALL IT THE **METRO MAP**!
WE WERE KIND OF HOPING FOR THE WHEEL, BUT ACTUALLY THIS LOOKS FAR MORE USEFUL!
Q5
Kerber

'You ought to dream. All our biggest businessmen have been dreamers.'

— Ernest Hemingway, *The Sun Also Rises*

Joe Reade
John Varvatos
Mike Soutar
Alan Rusbridger
Deborah Turness

QUARTER TWO

2012–2015 The Sun Also Rises

Q5
NEW YORK
OFFICE OPENING!!!
WHAT THE HELL IS ORGANIZATION DESIGN? ...WE ONLY DO ORGANISATION DESIGN!
KESTER

From the frugal years that followed the Global Financial Crisis, in London the 2012 Olympics seemed to mark the beginning of a more positive, optimistic outlook. At Q5 we saw a gradual change in the work we were doing from a cost-cutting focus to work more focused on driving growth for our clients. We opened our first international office, in New York.

For the Island Bakery, it was the year they impressed Marks and Spencer with their commitment to renewable energy, producing organic biscuits on the Isle of Mull. In his interview, the Island Bakery founder and CEO, Joe Reade, tells us how they grew the business, and about his experience on Dragon's Den.

We also hear from two entrepreneurs. John Varvatos launched his eponymous brand with seven or eight people. Now, there are 400 employees around the world. Mike Soutar has a similar story of success as Stylist magazine, which he founded in 2009, went global.

Will Lewis (News Corp), Alan Rusbridger (Guardian) and Deborah Turness (NBC) describe how they have plotted their paths through the media, and share their thoughts and experience of the current, seemingly endless, disruption of the industry.

If you're proud of it and you do it well, everything else will fall into place. Profit and money are an objective way to measure the success of a business, but it shouldn't be the only thing you try to achieve.

Joe Reade

POSITION AT TIME OF INTERVIEW:
CEO of The Island Bakery, Organic Food (Scotland)

Joe Reade is the co-Founder and CEO of The Island Bakery, which makes arguably the most delicious organic biscuits in the world.

Born in Somerset, Joe moved the Hebridean Island of Mull as a teenager. After graduating with a degree in Edinburgh, Joe started his bakery business with his girlfriend (now wife) Dawn, in a garage on the Isle of Mull. It was the early 1990s, and neither Joe or Dawn knew very much about baking bread.

In this interview, twenty five years after launching the business, Joe talks about how he took the company from one that baked loaves of bread for the tiny population of Mull to a business that supplies high-end biscuits across the UK and Europe, to the likes of British Airways and Marks & Spencer. All this despite failing to win financial backing on the TV show, Dragons' Den...

What was the driving force in you moving back to Mull after university?
It started with a very simple and naïve idea that we would bake bread and sell it on our island. My family moved to Mull when I was 12; we were a family of dairy farmers. My dad was a great romantic and he wanted to sell his milk to people rather than have it trucked away to someone anonymous.

He dragged us and his cows to the Isle of Mull when this derelict farm became available, and we started milking cows and delivering the milk door-to-door. The family started making cheese to balance the supply and demand of milk; you can't turn cows' udders on and off like a tap, so milk got made into cheese, and that's Isle of Mull cheese. Over the years, the cheese became much more successful than the milk.

After university in Edinburgh, I came back home wondering what on earth to do with my life. The only thing I did know was that I wasn't going to have a job. My dad was quite entrepreneurial and imaginative, a first-generation farmer. He was quite an odd bod to be a farmer. I had grown up thinking that I couldn't imagine a son of Jeffrey Reade working for someone else.

Did you go to the Milkrounds (university jobs market)?
No, I was a naïve farmer's boy; I didn't know what all the options were for a graduate. I just assumed that I would do something on my own. I spent a year mucking about on the farm, then a local baker was retiring, and it was suggested by my mother that I look at taking on his bakery. She wanted her son to stay close by!

Had you ever baked bread before?
No, I'd never baked a loaf of bread in my life! I thought it could work well because my family were delivering milk, and that was as far as the business planning went. If I'd got safe and secure in a job, I would never have done it, as you don't want to lose that security net of a safe salary. The only time I've had a wage was when I worked in a fish and chip shop when I was 16.

Did you have to make a large capital outlay when you launched?
It was pretty modest. In 1994, we took out our first overdraft, and debts have only ever grown since, which has been fun! I'd had a small amount of money that I'd inherited from my grandmother who'd had a bit of land. She had some allotments in Somerset. They got sold off and houses were stuck on them. My share of that was £17,000 and I used that money to buy the oven.

My brother had just moved into a new house and he had a big garage on the end; a big domestic garage where the owner kept two or three cars. We said, 'Could we have that for our bread baking please?'

Through the Isle of Mull cheese links we had, I went to spend a week learning to bake in a bakery in Oxford. Through another friend on Mull, I spent a few days in a bread baking college in Portsmouth. I learnt the basics, the rudiments of how to bake bread. I bought a mixer and, over a few tables, started baking bread and selling it around the island. Our bread could be as awful as you like because we were the only bakery, so we got away with being quite bad at the beginning. Had we had competition, I'm sure we wouldn't have fared as well!

Did you share distribution with the family dairy business?
We would bake bread through the early hours of the morning, through the night. Vans from the farm would come after loading up with milk; they would load up with bread and take it around the island, delivering it to all the shops and doorsteps throughout the morning. That was the model. It's the oldest, most basic, rudimentary business model there is; produce food and sell it to people. We weren't breaking any moulds, we weren't a disruptive business, we were just providing a service in a place where there wasn't one and doing it in a place where I happened to live.

You must have been getting up in the early hours every day, which must have been gruesome at times. Is it easy to look back now and romanticise about it?
It was fun and exciting, but it was also bloody hard work. There were a few times where the memory of being a carefree student was still fresh in the mind, yet here Dawn and I were on the Isle of Mull working a night shift, baking bread through the night. There were aspects of it that I'll always remember fondly, such as the insect life we would see collecting on the window, attracted by the light of the bakery in the middle of the Scottish night.

Early on you started being quite opportunistic and spotting gaps in the market locally. Was this the first phase of growth?
The local business is difficult – not just because it's small – but because it is so seasonal. In the winter there are only 2,000 people on Mull. In the summer, we've got a population of about 9,000 in total, with the influx of tourists. The simple idea behind producing biscuits was that we would make something that was high value with a longer shelf life that we could send further afield.

Was this the point at which you started getting involved in branding and marketing?
We'd always had a reasonable eye for, and an appreciation of, branding and marketing, particularly Dawn. There was a gap in the market for

decent organic biscuits; organics were surging at the time. The most obvious competitor product was Duchy Original. We thought, 'Goodness if they can sell their biscuits for *that* much money, we could surely make something better and command the same price!'

Talk a little more about the branding you came up with.
It can't be hollow and empty. We are authentic in that we are a little manufacturing business run by myself and my wife trying to make nice stuff in the world of fine food. There are lots of made-up brands that are the product of a brainstorming session in a branding agency. These guys are trying to extract and create a brand out of nothing. There's either no authenticity or they're trying to find a nugget of authenticity in what otherwise might be a bland and uninteresting story. I'd like to think that, although The Island Bakery is a nice brand, it's also reflective of the trust and essence of what we are, which is a small and friendly bakery on the Isle of Mull.

What's been the biggest challenge for you as a business?
I think probably my own personal development. It's recognising what I'm good at and what I'm not so good at and understanding what I'm best using my time for and what I'm not. I have had to learn how and when to bring other people into the business as this thing has grown. There are a lot of logistical and practical problems that come with running a business on Mull, but my development has been my biggest personal challenge.

As the company evolves, is it growing every year?
Yes, pretty much, but not every year. 2008 was a bad year. As the credit crunch kicked in, people stopped buying expensive biscuits. It's pretty tough at the moment; butter has doubled in price and chocolate has become more expensive because of the poor exchange rate. So, we've suddenly found our margins wiped out by ingredient inflation, which is taking some time to overcome. So, we're growing in capability, in what we do and experience, but not always growing in sales. It doesn't always follow a nice smooth linear path; it goes up and down, but the general path is up. We've now got about 40 employees, all on Mull. We've moved out of that little garage that we borrowed from my brother and built a big bakery.

At the time, we thought it was enormous but now we're bursting at the seams and desperate to add on to it. We're one of the bigger businesses on Mull. We're one of the few that provide stable year-round employment and that's something to be proud of.

How do you get attention from the likes of Marks & Spencer (M&S)?
We don't have a sales or marketing department, and we don't have someone who goes out knocking on doors. We rely a great deal upon the product selling itself. The British Airways (BA) business is a good example of that. We got rung up one day, because the person that looked after the menus at BA had eaten our biscuits – bought from a deli – and thought they were lovely. So he asked if we could supply them.

We went to M&S because at the time they were just getting to grips with what they called their 'Plan A' programme, which was the head of M&S's big initiative at the time. It was their environmental programme through which they were trying to decrease the business' carbon output, reduce packaging and generally become more ethically, environmentally and socially conscious.

One of our USPs when we built our new bakery was not just that we were making organic biscuits, but that we wanted to extend that principle by baking using wood that is carbon neutral. We were taking trees that had absorbed carbon as they'd grown on Mull. There are lots and lots of trees; commercial plantations that normally go for paper. We buy a small portion of that and heat our oven with it. That was another nice aspect of the brand alongside the organic thing. We thought that it would be a good story for M&S and that it would suit M&S with their Plan A aspirations.

What prompted you to go onto Dragons' Den?
That was just a curious bit of fun around the time we were trying to raise money for our new factory. We were in a borrowed space in my brother's garage and we wanted to build a 600 square metre factory and equip it. It was very difficult to raise the money. During the process of trying to raise funds, I was at a trade show in Glasgow, standing in my little booth, trying sell biscuits. Dragons' Den had a team of researchers there. They approached me and asked if I would fill in an application form. I filled the form in and got to go onto Dragon's Den. I had no desire or intention to get investment from them because I really didn't want to do it that way. I wanted to borrow the money because that's the cheapest way to borrow, from a bank. It was really just a bit of fun and an experience.

Would you recommend the experience?
I wouldn't recommend doing Dragons' Den to anyone who's doing it for the money, because then it's going to be torture. It's not a real business pitching environment, it's a television programme.

I was really nervous about the whole thing. I used to do a bit of amateur dramatics when I was younger and whenever I was very nervous my top lip would start to quiver and twitch. I would find myself chasing my top lip up as I tried to control it and my head would start to tilt back. I was terrified that this was what was going to happen to me on telly, so I took some Beta blockers to help calm my nerves and keep my heart rate down. I took two while we were waiting to go on. I'd been taking half of one every couple of hours. We got a 30-minute warning, so I downed two more of them and went into the studio. It was the most bizarre experience. I had the heart rate of an elderly elephant and I was completely unphased and unstressed about the whole thing. It was like I was in a weird dream; I knew I should be nervous and anxious, but I wasn't. I came across as a complete buffoon, I think!

Do you have a personal motto that you live your life by?
My dad used to say, 'If it needs advertising, it's not worth buying!' and I always thought that was a stupid thing to say. But it's true that if you can produce a good product, people will come to you to an extent. So, have faith in your products, I would say.

What advice would you give to the Generation Zs?
If you're proud of it and you do it well, everything else will fall into place. Profit and money are an objective way to measure the success of a business, but it shouldn't be the only thing you try to achieve.

Interview: OP, London

We weren't breaking any moulds, we weren't a disruptive business, we were just providing a service where there wasn't one and doing it in a place where I happened to live.

You can have a dream, it is the greatest thing to have the dream – the success, though, is being able to execute it.

John Varvatos

POSITION AT TIME OF INTERVIEW:
Founder, Chairman & Chief Creative Officer of John Varvatos, Fashion (Global)

John Varvatos' family originally hails from the village of Poulata in Greece, although John was born in Detroit, and grew up in Allen Park, Michigan.

Since the launch of John Varvatos in 2000, the company's founder and namesake has gone from strength to strength. Winning CFDA Menswear Designer of the Year and a partnership with Converse early on, John has since expanded his business across the U.S. and been named GQ Designer of the Year. In 2012, John joined the cast of celebrity mentors on NBC's Fashion Star, a reality competition series that searches for the next big brand in fashion. We interviewed John in 2015, about becoming a global brand and his resolve to 'always be a sponge'.

In recent years, John has focussed on his customers' online experience, teaming up with Salesforce to curate a luxury digital shopping experience. John is dedicated to ensuring that 'customers can have an immersive, personal experience online just as they would in-store.'

What was the spark that made you set up your own business?
In New York at the end of '98/'99, everything seemed to be black and everything seemed to be nylon. It was Prada, Gucci, Hugo Boss and Jil Sander. They are great brands but there was a lot of similarity in this minimalist modern look. I thought, what a great time to do something completely different. So, it was one of those impulsive things that happened very quickly; someone who had approached me previously backed me financially and within a week we'd put everything together.

What was fundamental to your success in the first year?
We had a very clear vision of what the brand stood for – what the product was. When we launched, the reception was phenomenal. One thing that really stood out was our people, and the key word in the first year was 'execution'. I was not 25 years old; I was 43 when I started the company and there was a big difference in terms of understanding what it takes to execute versus just dreaming. A lot of young brands starting up – they have the idea, but they stumble in the execution.

You are a global brand, opening new stores across the UK, Asia and Europe. How does this growth shape your view of the future?
When we started the company, we had 7 or 8 people. Today we have 400. As you grow the main challenge is maintaining the culture in order to find and keep great people. The exciting part of it is we have not even scratched the surface. We see so much opportunity both internationally and domestically here in the US. Of course, it's weighted with its own challenges, which is what we spent time with you [Q5] on. Sometimes you can run too fast and I think if we've stumbled at all it has been due to running fast and pushing hard.

Are there any other organisations you look at that have grown as global brands and you think, they have done it right?
In our industry, the one brand that I look to that I think has done a great job of branding, marketing, and digital communications (which is huge in our world today) is Burberry. It is not a new brand; it is a very old brand that has been revived in the last 15 years. It was a very staid, old English brand that was tired and over licensed, and now they are the most desirable and innovative. They are the best for sure in terms of being in touch with the consumer – of any brand in the world for me.

What have been the biggest threats to maintaining the John Varvatos brand as you expand?
There is always the motivation to grow and sometimes step into broader areas that are not brand appropriate just because they are big wins. As the gatekeeper, I need to decipher what is really 'brand appropriate' and what could be detrimental in the long-term. What happens to a lot of brands as they grow is, they are driven by the business plan and the

top and bottom line growth. They start to do some things to drive the business that are not necessarily long-term strategies and can hurt the brand.

Who have been your biggest inspirations and influencers throughout your career?

When I was growing up, the fashion influence was on two different ends of the spectrum. There was Steve McQueen, who was effortlessly stylish. Then there were people like Jimmy Page or Jimi Hendrix who were less effortlessly stylish, but very, very cool in their own right. Then there were the business influencers. Peter Strom (President of Ralph Lauren) and then Ralph himself. They couldn't have been more different people. Peter had everything from good business sense and business acumen to balls, whereas the thing that I learnt from Ralph is lead and never follow. Ralph was a total inspiration for me. His success has been clarity. He was so focused on clarity of vision – clarity of brand and story and he has never varied from it. There were no lifestyle fashion brands before Ralph Lauren. When I left Ralph Lauren, he said to me, if you really believe in your heart that you really, truly have something new to say, then you have my blessing. So, when I see him now, he will say 'he's really doing it, he really has something new to say'.

What would be your words of wisdom to someone starting out today?

Always be a sponge, just suck up as much information around you as possible. Get yourself involved in all aspects of it. I'm in my late 50s and I continue to learn something every day. Every time I hire somebody, they automatically think they should be running the place. I like that kind of mentality, but at the same time, they also need to understand that it is all about execution. You can have a dream, it is the greatest thing to have the dream – the success, though, is being able to execute it.

Interview: AC, New York

We try and make sure that the best argument wins, and that people don’t just salute whoever is in charge.

Mike Soutar

POSITION AT TIME OF INTERVIEW:
Founder & Chairman of Shortlist Media, Publishing (UK-based)

Mike Soutar was born in Dundee. Energetic, charismatic, and proudly Scottish, he has spent most of his career working in London.

In 2007, Mike co-founded Shortlist Media, the 'freemium' publisher of free weekly magazines (Shortlist and Stylist). The company grew to employ hundreds of people and generate revenues of more than £25 million a year.

We interviewed Mike in 2012, when both magazines were growing in revenue. Mike stepped down from the business in 2018, a couple of years after selling it. In 2019, Mike was appointed as Chief Executive of the Evening Standard.

Mike is also familiar to fans of UK version of the TV show, The Apprentice, as one of Lord Sugar's fearsome interrogators, when the hapless candidates get their often-flaky résumés ripped to shreds.

But we're not interested in Apprentice candidates here. We're interested in Mike himself, and his experiences with ShortList and Stylist. In this interview, Mike discusses the shift from a corporate to entrepreneurial mindset, and his advice for any young professional looking to 'start from scratch'.

What made you decide to pursue 'freemium' magazines?
Firstly, we were fascinated by the 'power of free' and how access to free entertainment had changed so much of the media world. It was changing newspapers with Metro and we were interested in seeing if the freemium model could work with magazines. Secondly, we looked into men's magazines, a struggling and declining sector, to try and work out whether men had been turned off magazines or whether magazines just weren't right for them. We were convinced it was the latter, so we put the two things together.

How did you approach getting your product 'out there'?
Getting a great distribution person was an early and important hire because nobody had ever tried to create a nationwide distribution network before. Metro had done it, but on a city-by-city basis with a couple of years in between each launch, and they are, in effect, regional editions. Nobody had ever tried to set up a hand distribution network outside London that involved distributing the same edition nationwide.

Did you trial or did you jump straight in?
We couldn't have completed the magazine, handed it out, and then assessed the impact as a trial run because we would have had no advertising backing. The business plan had to be an act of faith because the advertisers needed commitment from us in order to enable the business.

What was the shift like from being a director in a company to using entrepreneurial savvy at ShortList Media?
On the board at IPC (which later become Time Inc), I always had an insurgent mindset. When you're in a big company it's useful to try and think like an outsider because it's easier to take creative risks and consider big leaps of imagination. In the last three years I was at IPC we created four new magazines – 'Nuts', 'Pick Me Up', 'TV Easy' and 'Look'. I had already started to move out of a corporate mindset and into something more enterprising.

Were you seen as a bit of a rebel in your days at IPC?
I'd like to think my colleagues on the board realized that I was doing what was absolutely necessary in order to get us to a point where we would have some transformative launches. Fostering a spirit and provocative sense of independence was really important because until I did that, IPC hadn't launched anything successfully for 10 years. I was possibly a bit of an insurgent!

Recognising your insurgency back in those days, how would you tolerate that within your own business now?
I think that constructive dissent is the best thing you can have within a creative business. We try and make sure that the best argument wins, and

that people don't just salute whoever is in charge. We are always there for challenging ourselves and challenging our people, so we try and foster a culture where people from the grassroots upwards are empowered to ask questions. You're always looking to highlight your heroes and champion people who've done things in an innovative way.

Was launching *Stylist* a pre-planned decision or did it just seem like the obvious next step?

ShortList was always a starting point and it gave us various options. We decided it would be the start to our portfolio of premium print titles and associated digital platforms when we realised how difficult it had been to create a nationwide distribution network. We also had relationships in the market and a growing demand from women for an empowering, intelligent magazine that embraced a sense of modern, independent feminism.

How long did it take from securing investment to producing Stylist?

It took about nine months and we launched Stylist almost exactly two years after ShortList. We could have done it in about four if we had been under pressure to do so. But whilst ShortList was moving rapidly towards breakeven, when we first went to see our investors it hadn't reached that point yet so I think it was right that we didn't try and rush people into that decision.

When you set up ShortList you had four founders and within 20 months you had 95 employees. What pressure does that put on you and your founders?

It still surprises me that when I look around; it doesn't quite feel real because it's happened so quickly. We're now at 120, in six months' time we'll be 150-160. To cope with this, over the last year I've set up new starter lunches every couple of months to find out who everyone is.

What are your next steps for ShortList Media?

We see growth domestically, digitally and internationally. Our ability to make proper, sustainable returns from our digital ventures has really improved over the last 18-24 months. We have been infused with a greater sense of ambition and the confidence to go to our board of investors and ask to use our generated capital to reinvest in new launches. Hopefully we'll also have our first international edition soon. We're looking for a company that has the same appetite for risk that we do.

What could big publishers learn from your experience at ShortList?

When you start from scratch, you get an amazing opportunity to put things in place where you want them. Our philosophy, our cost base, our overheads and our overall approach were absolutely of the moment. As an insurgent, you are quicker, more flexible and adaptable and closer to the marketplace, so you must play to these strengths. However, when you're trying to improve an existing company it's more painful, difficult and costly because you can't just start from scratch. An incumbent has great power but is inherently slower. It is a privilege to start from scratch, so I wouldn't criticise anybody who's trying to steer one of the bigger companies round because that takes such effort.

What advice would you give to a budding entrepreneur who wants to start something from scratch?
You've just got to crack on and do it. Your first idea doesn't have to be your best idea and what you don't know is as important as what you do know. You also need real clarity of thought and purpose because as soon as you start, people and opportunities will distract you very quickly. You need to be single-minded. One of the biggest lessons I ever learnt was that investors back people first and ideas second. Ideas change because marketplaces and conditions change. At the end of the day, the investor values your commitment to the endeavour.

Finally, who is or are the biggest influences on your career?
I was very inspired working with Felix Dennis and I really took a lot out of working with Sly Bailey at IPC when she was the CEO. Sly was brilliant at the word 'no', which I'd never really learnt before. I've worked with all sorts of genius magazine makers including Marcus Rich at FHM, who taught me as much about analysing success as analysing failure. I still work with some people I admire enormously, including all the ShortList founders and our inspiring Chairman Sir David Arculus.

Interview: OP, London

I think that constructive dissent is the best thing you can have within a creative business.

In one sentence, when I did succeed, it was as a result of unleashing the creativity and cleverness in others. You cannot be a good leader if you feel threatened by other bright people.

Alan Rusbridger

POSITION AT TIME OF INTERVIEW:
Outgoing Editor of The Guardian, News Publishing (UK-based)

Editor-in-chief of the Guardian for twenty years, Principal of Lady Margaret Hall (LMH), at the University of Oxford, board member of the National Theatre, author, screenplay writer, regular writer for the New York Review of Books – these are just a few of the posts that Alan can lay claim to.

Considering all this, it is difficult to believe that Alan was never 'the brightest boy at school or university' - but that, he claims, was the bedrock of his achievements. 'When I did succeed, it's as a result of unleashing the creativity and cleverness in others.'

Born in Lusaka, in what is now Zambia, we spoke to Alan shortly after he stepped down from his stellar career at The Guardian. It was in 2015, shortly after he had begun his new role at LMH.

Since our interview, Alan has been appointed as chair of the Reuters Institute for the Study of Journalism and authored another book, 'Breaking News: The Remaking of Journalism and Why It Matters Now'.

Alan, what was the initial spark that made you want to go into journalism?

I grew up reading newspapers because my father was obsessed with them. I wrote to the local paper, the Surrey Advertiser, who took me on for some work experience. From day one I thought it was the best, most fun and interesting job you could possibly do. So that was it.

Who have been your biggest inspirations and influencers throughout your career?

When I properly started in journalism, I was with the Cambridge Evening News and in need of having the smooth edges knocked off me a bit. There is nothing quite like working for a local newspaper to do that; in particular, nothing quite like working for a big, tough Glaswegian wearing dark glasses and smoking a cigar. Fulton Gillespie was the Chief Reporter on the Cambridge Evening News. He took the Cambridge-educated, English Literature graduate and taught him how to 'write tight', to be cheeky, nosey and intrusive - all things journalists have to be. There were other people too like Harry Evans, Peter Preston and Nick Davies, all great journalists and people who inspire me.

You were at the helm of The Guardian for two decades. What was your leadership philosophy?

Well, I was never the brightest boy at school or university and certainly not at The Guardian either. I was surrounded by incredibly bright people and because The Guardian does not have a proprietor, you do not look up at anybody. Your only relationship is with your colleagues. So, there is much more of a lateral structure in place. I think you must have the confidence to share responsibility, ideas and decision-making with these incredibly bright people, whilst not being insecure or too controlling. This brings out the best and the most creative qualities in them. In one sentence, when I did succeed, it was as a result of unleashing the creativity and cleverness in others. You cannot be a good leader if you feel threatened by other bright people.

The Guardian embraced the digital world early on. How did you educate your colleagues into thinking that digital was a place where people should want their voice, words and stories heard?

That was a huge challenge. With 600 journalists, there were both hares and tortoises. There were people who absolutely did not believe in 'digital', who felt threatened by it, and did not want to move. And others who believed that if you didn't move in the next five minutes, never mind the next 5 hours or next 5 days, you were going to be left behind. One of the skills in leadership is keeping everybody together. I have seen lots of newspapers break in half by not being able to keep people in the same caravan. You can have a loose caravan whereby people move at different paces, but they somehow must all move together. The other challenge is being in a situation where you cannot provide definitive answers. You can't stand up in front of 600 people and promise them that everything will be alright. You are, after all, making your best educated hunch at the way the world will go; but nevertheless, you have to get everyone to buy in to that. The only way I could encourage people to do that was by getting people together in groups and setting them the same dilemma that was rattling around in my own head. Nearly always the groups would arrive at the same conclusions that I had. The value was not necessarily that everyone would agree with you, but that they could see and follow the thought process behind the decision.

You moved The Guardian out of some rather antiquated and messy offices in Farringdon to the modernity of Kings Place. Looking back, was that new environment something that helped you drive rather more sweeping change at the guardian?
Well it is one of those mantras of change; if you only change the building and do not use it as a vehicle for other forms of change then you have wasted an opportunity. You can only do other forms of change if you do something symbolic, like move into a brand-new building. We got to the situation where there were four bits to The Guardian including the daily print, the weekend print, The Observer and digital. Each had their own structure, leaders and processes, housed in 6 different buildings and we could not progress in the physical structures we were in. So, moving to one modern building presented an opportunity to bring everyone together. It was not just about seating plans but about the fundamental relationships between these four different groups of people and integrating them into a streamlined collective that was able to work together.

So, the move to Kings Place was culturally significant?
It was a huge thing because of the different cultures. You had a group of people working on a Sunday paper who had seven days to think about stories and who really did not, at that point, have to think about digital at all, sitting alongside people whose time spectrum might be a minute. It was crucial to unify those people with a common sense of what *The Guardian* and *The Observer* were going to be. Through having those conversations, which were, at times, painful and laborious, we were able to craft something that we felt might work. But that was never going to be permanent because nothing ever is. A lot of the structures that we agreed on and designed turned into floorplans; a few were unpicked within months, others a year later. Either way, it enabled us to go into Kings Place in an agreed way, with everyone feeling that they had been treated fairly, like they had some agency in it. If we had not got that right, we would still be arguing about it today and thus be very dysfunctional. The fact that we did get that right enough meant that we moved much faster than other news organisations that perhaps had not grasped that point.

When you started your editorship, The Guardian was very much a UK-based news organisation, but over course of the past few years it has invested in operations around the world. How have you gone about extending The Guardian's influence and reach? Has it been problematic?
Well if there was a metaphor for that, my wife has just got into bread making. Bakers carry around little pots of Baker's yeast .... disgusting stuff! Our pot lives in the kitchen on the shelf. Some bakers have pots that go back hundreds of years; you can remake it and adjust the ratios. I think you need a bit of that. You can buy office space in New York and stick *The Guardian* on the door, but you need some of this *Guardian* yeast to start the culture, which then makes it *The Guardian*. You have to have enough brilliant people from the guardian, who can then go and work with Australians or Americans and spread that this is how the guardian actually is. Then suddenly within a year you have something that is recognisably the guardian ... you have this beautiful loaf. There were a couple of false starts where we did not have the right mix, or we didn't have enough guardian-esque-ness in it. This brought some difficult decisions as to how much you do from the centre versus how much you can delegate and how you define the decisions that need to be taken from the centre. It is quite challenging moving up in scale but if you get it right then it is hugely exciting.

**In recent years, the big stories that The Guardian have broken and 'owned' have been international ones.
This is a bit of a shift too isn't it?**
It is the nature of the world and communication. *The Guardian* saw its fate as being international, so we increasingly did stories that had international ramifications. Partly it is just globalisation itself; if you live in London, Singapore or Mumbai, your life does not make sense as a closed, sealed bubble. There is so much going on with security, religion, the environment and economics that is going to impact your lives that, in a way, you cannot make sense of the world unless it is reported internationally.

Newsrooms tend to be rather short-termist; many businesses are like this too. How did you encourage longer term thinking? For instance, you spent much of your final year talking about big issues like climate change...
Well I think it is something that the media can and should do. It is quite hard for politicians to be long term, as they have to focus on getting elected. So, something that has to be thought of as a 20 or 30 year problem is difficult for politics; but it shouldn't be for news organisations because we don't have to get elected. Nevertheless, I think a lot of media is short term obligated, "of the minute".

…. such is the 24/7 rhythm of the newsroom?

Yes, and journalism was failing with Climate Change because, almost by definition, the story does not change much day to day. I mean there may be an iceberg melting that has lost a millimetre in Greenland but journalism thrives on novelty and things that are happening, more reportable matters. It is difficult to evaluate the risks of something that might happen in 35 years. However, if journalists do not do that, they are not going to help politicians in taking the difficult decisions. Climate Change is one of those things I decided we needed to find more imaginative ways to get back into the debate.

The media world is full of 'shouty' editors. Did you ever raise your voice?

I cannot remember if I ever did, no. [Chuckles] No.

Looking back over your many years at the guardian, putting the stories to one side, what do you feel is your greatest achievement?

My tenure as editor of *The Guardian* coincided with a time where the economic model of the newspaper industry was under intense pressure. Everything was in flux. Yet we were able to keep our journalists together and focused on producing proper journalism across all platforms. Because of this, by the time I left, our audience had never been larger. The Guardian is in good shape to flourish for at least another generation.

And finally, do you still play the piano? Or did your year learning Chopin's Ballade a few years ago finish you?!

No, I very much enjoy the piano! It has been the thing that has kept me vaguely sane over the years.

Interview: OP, London

I think organisations should be places where there is a clear, deliberate, smart strategy in place. That strategy needs to be communicated to everybody. You have to focus on the goals.

Deborah Turness

POSITION AT TIME OF INTERVIEW:
President of NBC News International (France / UK-based)

Born in Hertfordshire, Deborah Turness studied French and English at university, before taking a postgraduate course in Journalism at the University of Bordeaux.

After an intoxicatingly fun internship at ITN, Deborah began her career at ITV, and became the first female Editor of ITV News in 2004.

In 2013, Turness was appointed President of NBC News, subsequently becoming President of NBC News International. Earlier in her life, she was reportedly expelled from her convent school for kissing a boy.

Married with two daughters, Deborah seems to work 100 mph, yet still finds time to do up houses in her spare time.

What first excited you about journalism?
My family always had the news on. I remember watching the television coverage of the Heysel stadium disaster, rooted to the spot, watching something truly terrible unfold. Even then it struck me: the mighty responsibility on journalists having to tell this story, as it unfolded right in front of them.

I was always interested in current affairs at school. I launched a Schools Page in the local newspaper, *The Stevenage and Hitchin Gazette*; myself and a friend were reporters. I also did a summer job working for the local paper when I was 15 or 16.

I progressed to writing music reviews. I figured that if I wrote about bands, I'd get into gigs for free, get to meet the bands and interview them! Then, when I went to college in London, I continued doing music reviews for the London Student magazine and began building plans to launch a college campus radio station.

The real change in my life was doing a French and English degree. My French media tutor knew the person who ran the school of journalism at the University of Bordeaux. He asked if I'd like to go and do a post-grad course in journalism there. I said, "I'd love that!"

Was this course in French?
Yes, I was doing a French degree. I have French connections in my family, so my French was good. By the time I'd finished my fourth year, I had not only got my degree, I had completed my post-grad course. At that point, it was necessary to do an internship. So, I did mine at ITN's office in Paris. I made some great contacts there. The then Bureau Chief, Barbara Grey, gave me my first big break.

I called ITN. Barbara said that the office was in the basement of her house and she needed to clear out her files. She said that if I didn't mind doing that for nothing, I could come and work with her for a week. As it happened, I didn't end up clearing her files. Two big stories broke that week. I was able to show her how useful I could be doing interviews, researching, making phone calls and booking interviews. So, she invited me back to be a junior researcher and producer for the upcoming French election, which was Chirac versus Mitterrand. She paid my train fare, and I was up and running. That was my biggest breakthrough.

Were there other guiding lights in your early years?
Barbara opened the door for me. Jon Snow was also massively helpful. His producer fell ill, during that election, and I ended up picking up this work. He sent me to an event the night before the election to try to get Chirac. I managed to corner Chirac in a Mairie [the town hall] and

asked him a load of questions. There were no other journalists there, and it was lead story on the *News at Ten*.

It's worth adding, that I failed to get onto ITN training scheme. But Jon helped open the 'side door' for me. I ended up managing the people who had been on the training scheme that year. Things work out!

Have you found television news sexist in your career?
I don't feel proud that I'm the first female editor of a TV news operation in the UK and the US. I just think, what took them so long? Let's face it, it wasn't that long ago that I took over as editor of ITV news.

Television news was a very male-dominated environment when I got into it. Decisions were made in the pub. Predominantly women were desk assistants. There were a few incredible women who were thriving in senior roles. For instance, there was a female Director and Head of Foreign News. But I can count the senior women on one hand. It was very much a Boys' Club, which was inherently sexist. As a woman you had to be tough enough to work very hard and prove yourself much more than any equivalent guy. But I've always been very focused and had the capacity to work hard. I found, in a very strange way, that being in the minority served me well. I got noticed. People would say, 'Oh God, she can do *that*.' I would go out with news crews and travel to horrible places and do the most difficult things. I was always very conscious; I would think "Right, I'm going to pick up the very heavy BBW edit pack off the belt at the airport and put it on the trolley." I would play my part whether it was a war zone or an earthquake. It's the way I am anyway. If you show that you can play an equal role in the tough world of sharp-edged television news .... if you show that you can cut it, survive and thrive ...... it sets you up for the rest of your career.

How much of a plan did you have for your career? Or did you seize opportunities as they came along?
The majority of my career has been about doing a job well, so that the next door opens up for you. There have been points where I have been quite strategic. For example, when I was editor of ITV News, the role itself became more strategic. I started becoming much more involved in the commercial side. I went to Ashridge Business School and did their mini MBA for future leaders. It was one of the best things I'd ever done.
I would think strategically about business, about ad sales, about diversifying revenue streams etc. It took me to a different level. When NBC News approached me about becoming the President of NBC News, a role which involved running hundreds of millions of advertising sales, I was able to present a business plan for them. I understood the challenges the business had. I recognised the decline of the ad sales market. I quickly worked out the absolute necessity to diversify revenue streams, to drive growth and to transform the business. I knew what the underlying problems were with the business. Had I not been to Ashridge, I couldn't have done that.

Along that journey you will have had some challenges too. What are the biggest that you've had to confront in your business management career?
For me, my favourite type of challenge is taking a brand that's got legacy, history and value but has lost its way. I like to find a way to put that brand and their products back on track, to do a complete make-over. It's like renovating a house. I love to keep the bones of the house, cherish what's wonderful about the house, but completely transform it and to bring it up-to-date. I like to make it feel modern and fresh and relevant for now. NBC News was such a great organisation with great brands, hugely deep connections to its consumers, and enormous reserves of trust. But, in the competitive cut-throat world – and daily knife-fights – of American network TV, it had lost its way. I enjoy having that challenge of refreshing these brands.

I think the greatest challenge for me, and one that I hope I conquered, is to be the complete and ultimate outsider, brought into an organisation like NBC News, with a change mandate. I think it had to be an outsider that did that. I was deeply privileged to do it, with an organisation that big, with a heritage and history that long. Previous presidents had all come from inside. And there I was; not from NBC, nor another American network, not even an American, but a Brit. I had to work very hard to build relationships and to be trusted.

Would you say you're more of an agitator, a 'shaker upper' of a leader, than one that manages the status quo?
I wouldn't call myself a 'shaker upper'. I don't subscribe to the chaos theory. I think organisations should be places where there is a clear, deliberate, smart strategy in place. That strategy needs to be communicated to everybody. You have to focus on the goals. I'm going to come in and ask the consumer why this brand isn't working. It's my role to pull things together, to reshape things and rebuild in collaboration with the people who are doing it every day. Collectively, we are going to make it better, and know how to measure our future success.

But after that disruptive period of transformation, you need to focus solely on delivery and execution, and be able to measure that. There's a long tail when it comes to transformation, which can take two to three years. I enjoy that too. After that period, it probably needs to be reviewed. I think, if I'm honest with myself, while I don't want chaos, I will always continue to want to innovate, whether it is the journalism, storytelling, breaking boundaries or doing new things with tech.

You have been a big instigator of correspondents filming on smartphones. Tell us more about this.
Yes, right now I'm building this quite provocative position. At Euronews NBC [Deborah leads the International Operations], our politics trades

under a banner of being unapologetically impartial. We are the first major news operation to go 100% mobile phone. It's all mobile journalism, all the time. I have been a keen advocate of using mobile technology for years; whether it's the launch of a mobile phone network of journalists, or getting the tech in place to enable the ITV News to be beamed live from Antarctica. We had to ship a 30-metre dish out to do that! I like pushing boundaries.

Talking now about your new Raw Politics show, it has been observed that there are people who appear with uncomfortable far-right opinions on the show, such as Nigel Farage. Why don't you use this as a platform for individuals with progressive attitudes standing up for marginalised people?
I love this question. It goes to the heart of our strategy. If we don't have a platform where nationalists, populists, liberals, far-leftists have a debate or conversation, limiting ourselves to one side of today's divided politics, we will never solve the problems. We will become our own echo chamber. The whole point of what I'm trying to do with Euronews is to say Europe's people and politicians are divided, politics has gone tribal.

The easier divisions of politics of only a few years ago were mostly economic divisions. It's not like that now. It's about values and culture; you are anti-immigration and globalisation, anti-gay rights, anti-abortion, etc. It's about a set of values versus another set of values. Mainstream media has run into trouble because they have found it very hard to get their arms around the nationalist populist surge. Brexit won, in Germany the EFD have got a huge influence and larger share of the vote than they ever thought they would. In Italy the Lega and Five Star are running the country. And there's a complete deadlock in Swedish politics because nobody wants to do a deal with the far-right on the balance of power in traditional parties.

The word 'mainstream' has been come a 10-letter abbreviation for our failures: failure to see the populist revolution coming, failure to listen to the voices of the people who called for it and failure to adequately tell that story and fairly represent it on our platforms. Therefore, we should not be surprised to find that trust in 'mainstream' media is waning among certain groups. If we don't reclaim 'mainstream', we are going to consign ourselves to only being trusted by the half of the population that agrees with our views anyway. Nigel Farage effectively won Brexit, more people voted for Farage's point of view than didn't, so how do you even imagine there's a world where you can just ignore him?

The aspiration to be a trusted news provider is 100% trust over 100% of the population. The only way to do that and get those people back, is for them to feel convinced that you're an honest broker and you do not write them off as bigots. You give them respect for the fact that they're facing challenges, with immigration in communities and in their schools, and the fact that globalisation took jobs out of their job market. When you ignore people's points of view and their voices, when you try to silence them and marginalise them, they become even more angry and extreme.

I'm going to go onto some non-news related questions now. What advice would you give to Generation Zs starting out in business today?

Work harder than you probably think you're going to have to. We have some Generation Zs working on our politics show. I love this generation, and what makes them tick. We seem to have moved beyond the boozing lad and ladette culture and we're now in a more comfortable place that millennials have handed down. They care about the planet and about mental health.

I would also encourage them, if they can earn enough money to do so, to take a year off before you start working properly, to travel the world. There's such an obsession among people to go and explore the working environment. Of course, work is important, but we grow up in a very privileged world here and it's important to go see other societies before you start your career.

In the last 25 years of your career, have you been able to take off any chunks of time?

I've taken six months off for maternity leave twice. That was a journey into the real world for me; being around in the daytime hours, without having my head down in work mode, engaging with the NHS in a meaningful way. During my first maternity leave, I launched a business called *Digital Babies* with ITN – a platform for filming the answers to hundreds of questions that pregnant women and new mums and dads have. We filmed the answers with midwives, breastfeeding experts and paediatricians. I sold the idea into the NHS whilst I was on maternity leave. I loved doing that because it opened my eyes to a need out there. I would also say, as you embark upon a career, it's not about plan A because plan A often doesn't work; it's about having the capacity to find a great plan B.

Finally, on the topic of Generation Zs and 15 to 16-year olds, I read somewhere that when you were that age, you were expelled from convent school for kissing a boy? Is this topic off the menu?!

No, not at all! I was asked to leave a convent school at the age of 12. One of several contributing factors was that I smuggled some boys into the convent barn dance, which I thought would have made the school dance more fun. I was caught behind a bush by a nun. It was the last straw; there had been several incidents leading up to that!

Interview: OP, London

2012 AUSTERITY OLYMPICS
TOOTING LIDO
SORRY KIDS THEY RAN OUT OF MONEY, IT IS ONLY FOR THE NEXT 2 WEEKS!

‘Isn’t there something in living dangerously?’

— Aldous Huxley, *Brave New World*

Mark Scott
Darren Topp
Michael O'Keeffe
Matthew Crummack
Susanne Given
Alex Gourlay
Henry Ruiz

QUARTER THREE

2015–2018 Brave new world

EVERYONE IS TALKING ABOUT THE IMPORTANCE OF CULTURE......

Whilst we had been working with news publishing companies tackling digital disruption and the publication of their content for free across the globe since 2009, digital disruption had been a theme across most industries by this stage. And not just industry, listening to the people behind the Brexit vote in the UK, and those behind Trump's success in the presidential election in the US, it was clear they saw their digital strategies as key to winning those votes. It became a cornerstone of much of the work Q5 was doing around this time as well, not only in the UK and the US, but now in Australia too. In 2015, we opened the doors to our offices in Sydney and Melbourne. We speak to Mark Scott (Australian Broadcasting Corporation), Henry Ruiz (REA Group) and Matthew Crummack (lastminute.com and GoCompare) to whom digital disruption had presented some career highlights

We hear from several leaders in retail, a sector that is still working through how it addresses the threats and opportunities that digital brings. Darren Topp (BHS), Michael O'Keeffe (Aesop) and Alex Gourlay (Walgreens Boots Alliance) tell us about their careers in retail and beyond. Susanne Given (Chair of Made.com) talks about her experiences embracing digital retail. Some have thrived, some have just about survived, and one or two have experienced the bitter taste of failure.

There are plenty of lessons and pearls of wisdom for us all.

Don’t rush, take it easy, think it through and you’ll know it when you see it.

Mark Scott

POSITION AT TIME OF INTERVIEW:
Managing Director of ABC, TV (Australia-based)

Australian TV executive, Mark Scott, was appointed to his second five-year term as ABC's Managing Director in 2010. ABC, Australia's public broadcaster, went through transformational change under Mark's guidance. He cites the creation of iView as one of his 'happier' achievements. We interviewed Mark in his final year as Managing Director before going on to become secretary of the New South Wales Department of Education.

In this interview, Mark talks about why technology is such a 'massive driver', he outlines one or two of his regrets, relishes the challenges that he has embraced, and discusses the leadership style that has got him through it all.

How did you find moving from publishing to broadcasting?

My background was in news. News is a core part of what the ABC does. It gave me a good understanding of the culture that underpinned newsrooms. I had already experienced the changes that digital transformations brought to traditional media. There were a whole series of practical questions that I had limited understanding on; I had never worked in television, nor television production. The ABC had a lot of specialists in those areas I could draw on and who were generous with me.

The media industry is full of fiery leaders. What characterises your own leadership style?

I don't think I'm fiery or one of those 'type A chair-throwers'. I hope I'm respectful in my dealings with people, but at the same time, I understand how people need to work to deliver a strategic vision. I think I'm collegial. I'm a consensus builder. But that doesn't mean I see leadership as a popularity contest. People will back you, as long as they feel you are moving in the right direction.

How did you get your team to rally round your desire to embrace digital? Were there people that didn't get it?

The ABC had always had powerful content divisions, predicated around traditional platforms – radio and television in particular. I knew on arrival that convergence would be key. The ABC hero brand was so much stronger than the sum of its parts and would be even stronger if the divisions could work better together. That meant promoting the ABC executive as a whole and in a sense drawing power into some collective decision making at the centre. Some people struggled with that. Over time some of those people turned around and some left the organisation.

What were the biggest challenges you faced on the ABC digital journey?

When I started there was an innovative but small-scale digital centre, quite isolated from the real content machines. I devolved that group out to the content machines and we started getting good digital product progress. The weakness of that model is that those products don't really relate to each other and don't build the ABC digital experience as much as we need. In the absence of a digital rule book, are there organisations or individuals you look to for inspiration? I have gleefully watched and borrowed from whatever bright ideas I can find, including The Guardian, the BBC, the New York Times and National Public Radio. I've also had good conversations with Jeff Jarvis, Jay Rosen about the future of journalism and Tony Golsby-Smith about design thinking, human centred design and agile approaches to product development – all of which are now mainstream in what it is that we are trying to do here.

Any regrets with how you achieved what you have over the last 10 years?
I often think, why didn't we do this three years ago? But then you look back three years, you realise we were doing other important things. It took a while for us to be ready and ambitious enough to do it. We needed to define the burning platform to really engage people around the idea of a centralised ABC digital experience. If the executive was misaligned, we would never have been able to pull it off.

There are many things I'm sure you are proud of, but in your mind, what is your greatest achievement at the ABC to date?
One of my happier achievements was iView. I said to my team, 'I want one. You've got no budget. Now, off you go.' One team looked at the streaming model, one team looked at the download model and we ended up with a market leading product for years and years. I'm not sure if we'd thrown millions and millions at it, we would have got a better result.

What trends do you think the ABC will have to grapple with in the next 5 years?
Technology remains the massive driver. The hardware and software industries transform audience expectation. How much infrastructure we own and carry, how we use the cloud, how we use outsourcing. I think this will be pretty profound and fundamental.

What characterises the type of organisation you would see yourself working with next and why?
I was appointed here at what looks like a really young age. When I look back, I think about how I was only 43, and how brave that board was! Someone offering me a lot of money is not enough motivation as it turns out. I've got finite time; it needs to be something important and significant. It might not be in the media, there are other big interesting challenges out there. I've had some advice: don't rush, take it easy, think it through and you'll know it when you see it. And I'm, hoping that's right.

Interview: TL, Sydney

I believe the difference between 'good' and 'great' is motivation.

Darren Topp

POSITION AT TIME OF INTERVIEW:
CEO of LK Bennett, Fashion Retail (UK-based)

Darren Topp cut his teeth in the fast-paced world of Arcadia, before being appointed the CEO of BHS. Sadly for Darren, he was in charge of BHS when Dominic Chappelle acquired the business for £1 from Sir Philip Green. It was a very difficult time, and what happened next is well known. Darren has subsequently been the CEO of LK Bennett, and is currently the Chairman of Retail Executives.

When we caught up with Darren, he was happy to discuss any topic we could think of. In the interview that follows Darren shares his views on work, life and the future of retail.

How did you originally get into the world of retail?
It was completely by accident. At 15, I got a job on Salford Market selling jeans. This was at a time when everybody had 50 pairs of jeans. I loved it immediately and knew that this was an industry I could work in. I later got a Saturday job at Tesco and by then I was clear that retail was what I wanted to do. I applied for the Marks & Spencer management training scheme – and the rest, as they say, is history. I loved the excitement, the immediacy of it, how it was different every day. I fell in love with it overnight.

That Marks & Spencer scheme was quite renowned at the time – it was a big thing to get into.
It was. My mother was a cleaner at Marks & Spencer, so it was quite a big thing for me to be a management trainee. The company had a young management scheme, so I joined at 18. I didn't go to university. M&S was UK-famous, if not world-famous, for what many considered to be the best management trainee programme at the time. You did everything. The key to the scheme was that you swept the floor at night, you stacked the shelves, you did the whole lot. It put you in good stead for the future and many of the people on the scheme are the senior leaders in retail today.

What did you learn that has most carried you through to where you are today?
I think the basic principles of shop-keeping have been most important. You need to have decent products at a decent price, with good customer service. Yes, there are other things that are important – the store environment, the way in which you treat your people and the leadership qualities of the team running the business. But I think it was Simon Marks who said, 'good goods will sell arse upwards,' and he's probably not wrong. Having the right product is still a fundamental requirement of any retailer because, however good you are at running shops, however good the leadership team is, however good you are at merchandising, however good you are at the internet, at the end of the day, if the customer doesn't want it, they just don't want it.

You mentioned you didn't go to university. Did that affect how people saw you and has it affected you at all?
I don't think so. I think one of the great things about retail is that it is a meritocracy and I firmly believe that if you do a good job when you deliver, you will get recognised, you will get promoted and you can have a successful career. I buy the concept that there are certain careers where perhaps going to the right school or university or having the right qualifications matter disproportionately but, the truth is, retail is a business focused on results; it's a business that pays and promotes on results.

Why did you choose to leave Marks & Spencer?
I worked for Marks & Spencer until I was 39 so, after 20-odd years, I was an executive and I'd been pretty successful from a personal point of view. My ambition was always to be a store manager. I thought that if I could make store manager, I'd made it! You get a car and your own office. But I got to 39 and I just felt that the job wasn't stretching me anymore. I had a decision to make. Either I stayed and spent my time thinking about my pension and retiring, or I went and did something that would take me out of my comfort zone and stretch me in a different way.

What advice would you give someone starting out in retail today?
I think the first thing is you've got to have the retail bug. You've got to love the principles of retailing, customers, products and leading teams. Even in these difficult and challenging times, I still think it is one of the most rewarding careers anybody can have. It might not be the most financially rewarding but I think the combination of the work and genuine leadership skills is great. You've got people running single shops with a thousand people working there. These are big, big roles and I think they're demanding, stimulating and rewarding. And while retail is going through its version of the industrial revolution at the moment, I think it will come out stronger, fitter and better because it is full of people that genuinely care. As a country, we love going shopping, whether that's on the internet, in shops or via a magazine. That won't change but the current problems and challenges will.

How would you describe your leadership style or philosophy, and has it evolved through your experiences at BHS and LK Bennett?
It has certainly evolved, and I think one of the key criteria of any good leader is that there is no such thing as one-size-fits-all. My leadership style would be clear, supportive but demanding, yet done in a way that encourages people.

Who would you say have been the biggest influences on your career thus far?
I think my latter bosses at Marks & Spencer. From a leadership point of view, I learnt a lot from them and consider them to have a modern style of leadership. They influenced the way I operate and the way I lead, and I admired and tried to replicate some of their characteristics. Both of those guys, for example, were very inclusive, cohesive, engaging, believed in real two-way communication and listened.

And equally, people like Ian Grabiner (CEO of Arcadia), whom I learnt many things from. Ian's grasp of detail is a constant reminder to us all that however senior you are in an organisation you need to know what is going on.

I worked at Marks & Spencer when Stewart Rose was CEO and Charles Wilson was the CFO. There was a lot to admire in their leadership and the way in which they ran the business. They got people motivated around a common purpose. Philip Green. I admired his tenacious drive, his energy and his grasp of commercial detail. He kept you on your toes.

You took over BHS at a difficult time for the industry and the organisation. What are your reflections on how you led the company and your learnings from that experience?
I would like to start by saying I was genuinely honoured to be asked to run the business. It was a billion-pound business that had been losing money for a long time. It was a format that I think we could all recognise as very difficult. We knew that it was a tough gig in a good market, and this was a bad market. I went in knowing that and thinking I'm not going to sit in my office and watch the telly and smoke cigars and drink cups of coffee. This was going to be hard graft. We knew what we had to do, and we knew we had to do it against the backdrop of a very challenging market. We did a number of things that I believe, if we'd had the time and money, may well have saved that business. However, the rents and the rates in these businesses were horrific, which is why you're seeing a whole flurry of CVAs now.

Do you think there is a future for high street retail and, if so, what does that look like?
100%. I don't think it'll look significantly different from today. The challenge for retail structure is a combination of things we talked about such as rents, rates and the online business but we still spend 80% of our money in a shop. Most retailers don't want to close the shops, they just don't want to have shops that don't make any money. We had high streets in Roman times, and I think we'll have high streets in another 2,000 years. As a species, we want to meet people, get together, and have cups of coffee. So, while the makeup of it might change, I think it might become a bit more interesting. The 80s and 90s' growth in retail was such that high streets became a bit more homogenous and shops almost all looked the same. What you're getting now is creative entrepreneurs opening new, exciting, and interesting independent shops on high streets.

Then the LK Bennett opportunity came along. What went through your mind?
When you go through something like BHS, one of the things that goes through your mind is whether you will ever work again. I was genuinely concerned that, while I felt I had done a good job – if a good job could be done in those circumstances – maybe BHS would make me untouchable. The LK Bennett opportunity came along, and it was the first job I ever had where my wife said, 'You've got to work there. I love that brand!' So, I met the team at Phoenix.

LK Bennett is a super business in my view. Linda Bennett is remarkable and from a very select group of entrepreneurs that in the 80s, 90s and 00s had a real vision and passion for fashion and turned their enterprises into great businesses. Unfortunately for Phoenix, they bought it just before the financial crisis, which impacted everybody, and it impacted LK Bennett. Linda wanted to buy the business back. I think that was brave of Linda who certainly had an emotional attachment to that purchase. If you think about who is in the best place to ensure its survival, its growth and its success … Linda is that person.

If you were to advise someone who's taking on their first leadership or CEO position, what would you say?
People will do it in the way they think is right, and rightly so. If there was any advice, it would be to immerse yourself in the business quickly. It's easy to make comments from the cheap seats, outside looking in, but one of the key things for me is to get yourself around the organisation and talk to the customers, the staff, the team, the people who work there. Get a real sense of where it is because, the truth is, most people don't come to work to do a bad job, most people come to work and want to do a good job. I think making yourself accessible and listening early in your tenure as an MD or Chief Executive is really important.

Looking back on everything you've done, what are you most proud of?
Becoming store manager at Marks & Spencer was one of my proudest moments because it meant I hit a key goal. It was what I had set out to achieve. Then, equally, being made an executive, which was way beyond my expectations. That was very exciting.

Aside from technical experience, in terms of attitude and characteristics, what do you look for when recruiting a fresh graduate or experienced hire?
Once you get past the interest in retail, what you're looking for are people who are naturally inquisitive. Drive is also a big one for me – being driven to make things happen, to get things done. I believe the difference between 'good' and 'great' is motivation. For most jobs in the world, you don't need a first-class honours degree, but you do need to be able to coordinate, get things done, plan, organise and motivate people to do things, and to keep improving.

Interview: AC, London

You've got to work through and develop people, so that in an ideal world they can do it better than you. It's where you get long-term value.

Michael O'Keeffe

POSITION AT TIME OF INTERVIEW:
CEO of Aesop, Beauty retail (Australia-based)

Born in Australia, Michael O'Keeffe read Engineering and Computer Science at La Trobe University in Melbourne before moving into Marketing and Sales at Phillips. O'Keeffe then moved to London to do an MBA at London Business School. After stints in investment banking and consulting, he joined Aesop, the high-end beauty brand, as CEO, in 2003, turning it from a small wholesale business into a global retail chain with hundreds of stores across over 20 countries.

For O'Keeffe, values, culture and maintaining a distinct brand play an intrinsic part in Aesop's success.

What were the main drivers for you when deciding what you wanted to do as a career?
Having read engineering and computer science at university, I was attracted to problem-solving. From there I fell into project management. Mobile networks were starting to take off in Australia and globally and it seemed like an opportunity to problem-solve in an applied capacity. I didn't necessarily understand the world of business in terms of its functions but the complexity of problem-solving was very interesting.

So, with the background you had, what made you join Aesop?
It was a bit of a convoluted journey. I began working for Phillips and gained experience in dealing with Marketing and Sales. I then did an MBA at London Business School and this opened my eyes to the wider business universe and functions. I spent a few years in consulting and investment banking. I liked advisory and the intellectual capacity it required but I found I was losing the connection to product and building business. I was introduced to the founder of Aesop and immediately thought that it was a real business with some real products. I felt my career background in engineering meant I could make a real difference.

How did you go from a small-scale business to a successful global brand?
I think it is a combination of luck and good planning. We took it step-by-step. Very quickly, I understood that the main issues were on the front-end of the business. We had great products and an excellent brand, but people weren't connecting to it through wholesale. I had to transform the channel structure of the business in order to make that direct connection with the customer. Once we managed that, we started to scale up the front and back-end of the business through a continual, iterative process. We continually set a five-year plan, building value for the long term.

The brand has a very specific tone, look and authenticity, and it emphasises the importance of the core raw ingredients. How have you been able to maintain the brand as you have scaled up?
Often smaller niche brands are worried that the incumbents are going to move into their space but, in reality, most small niche brands actually transform and end up aligning themselves to incumbents. This is partly because the larger firms run their business model in a way that is proven to work at scale and partly due to human nature – an almost tribal, pack instinct, to drift across to the mainstream way of doing things. It's a corporate morphism – you get experienced people who have worked in the same industry and for the same companies, and industry regulation forces you to homogenise. But we don't want to be like the rest of the industry and use the same tools and branding.

What are the things you hold dear that stop you drifting across?
Firstly, it's important to recognise where differences lie and, for us, it's with our products, the creativity and design that imbues, and our customer service. Then you have to ask how you can make incredible customer service that works in one or two stores work in over three or four hundred stores across 22 countries. If you can solve that, it becomes a sustainable competitive advantage.

It's interesting you say that, because we often talk about how 'global' the world of business has become. Aesop is a global brand with a presence in multiple countries. Are there important factors that you have had to develop and maintain for local cultures to prevent the brand from being monolithically global?
Yes, particularly around customer-facing aspects. The beauty routine of a Korean customer who has seven or eight different skincare steps in the morning is very different to a British customer where you can barely get him or her to tone. In Asia, customers come into our stores and expect to sit down. However, a New York customer wants to be in and out as quickly as possible. You've got to have a core set of corporate values that are consistent. When we were younger, I think we tried to be too flexible from a country perspective. When we set up our Japanese subsidiary, I visited and found that it wasn't an Aesop business in Japan, but rather a Japanese business that just happened to do Aesop. That's the wrong way around. Instead, the core set of values and behaviours need to be consistent across the world.

In the global consumer market, we're forever hearing about the death of the high street. At the same time, we hear stories of new businesses that are doing particularly well. In terms of the beauty industry, what are the big trends or factors that you, as CEO, need to consider over the next five years?
Firstly, I think it is the concept of holistic care. People are just more aware and understand that beauty isn't just skin deep. It's in your nutrition, your lifestyle, the whole package. So, as a cosmetics company, how do we fit into that wider ecosystem? Secondly, the issue of personalisation – your consumers increasingly believe that they are a set of one, that their needs are unique. That runs contrary to general manufacturing and producing a product set. So how do the two mix? I have 150 hues, but complete customisation is a very different business model. Finally, the balance of products and services. Customers have enough material things. For a company that just produces products, it's a bit of a concern. You come to the question: do I want to produce services myself? It's a challenge.

Is that a USP, do you think? I.e. your ability as a smaller business to take a different level of risk?
Yes, and it's about understanding where you're taking risks too. It's not about taking risks on your back-end supply chain or your cashflow. The rest of the industry generally competes on product functionality or on celebrity endorsements. From my perspective, the products have to be great – particularly the ethics of skincare products, which are really important and lead to retention and loyalty. Above all, I want to create a unique brand that really connects to people on a deeper level. I want to compete by having incredible products as the base but increasingly elevate the brand to our purpose and what we stand for.

That moves us onto the conversation about culture. How have you invested in the culture and what have you done to grow it as you have grown as a brand?
Culture is really important. Your inside culture reflects on the outside. When there were 10 of us, located in one office, culture just built by being near each other. Now that we have more than a dozen offices scattered across the globe, it's a more directed internal communications programme or internal social media. The leaders of our organisation are always on the move around the different offices and engaging with people, and staff often transfer between offices. When new offices are set up, it should never be a completely new team, but should contain existing staff who understand the culture, values and behaviours. It's also about performance management and appraisal, not being results-focused alone.

What things as a leader are you really focused on in terms of driving the culture and what can you do to continually drive the right type of culture?
What I find is that an organisation can create silos very quickly; front-end, back-end, and also, silos between countries and regions. People tend to build their own chiefdoms vertically and think that as long as KPIs or SLAs between them are OK, then it works. Moving forward, the biggest problems we have are cross-functional or cross-regional. You need people to work together. Particularly with my leaders, I foster that perspective. If they're just looking down, this just builds through the rest of the organisation. It's critical that my team can look wider than just their own functional region.

Looking at your career to date, what is the thing that you are most proud of?
The overseas expansion. For any retailer, proving your concept in your own country is not easy but it's your home market. There are different rules and challenges offshore. We acquired our Japanese business from the distributer and it was a complete mess; culturally it was completely different. I moved over there and took my whole family. My children went to school in Tokyo. I spent two years turning that business around.

It allowed me to have a base in Asia and understand the Asian customer. We really proved ourselves – it made us confident that if we could make it in Japan, we could probably make it in most parts of the world.

If you were offering advice to someone who's starting their career, what would be the main tenants of that advice?
Firstly, I would say, slow down and take your time. Don't just think about how to climb the career ladder but think about how to build a base of different functions and regions. Early in your career, horizontal moves are just as important, or even more important, than vertical moves. I'd also say, whilst through university you are taught hard skills, the higher you go in your career the more it is the soft skills that make or break managers and leaders. What separates people as careers progress is the soft skills – empathy, ability to influence people, to get on with different cultures. Too many people push that aside for too long.

What is one of the hardest lessons you've learnt during your career?
That you can't do everything yourself. You've got to work through and develop people, so that in an ideal world they can do it better than you. It's where you get long-term value. Particularly as an entrepreneur, if you're doing everything yourself the business is either going to hit a ceiling very quickly or you will collapse.

You've gone from an organisation with 10 people to working in an organisation that recently became part of another company. You're part of a family of brands now. I imagine that changes a multitude of things for you as a leader and for the Aesop organisation. How have you found moving from an independent business to being part of a bigger, global family?
Internally, people were rightfully worried that we'd lose our independence and identity. The analogy that you use of a family is accurate – we're a family of businesses that have common attributes. We want to achieve something on the global stage, particularly demonstrating that capitalism and commercial businesses can be sustainable, positive forces in society. But, like any family, the individuals within it have their own identity and their own pathways. My job is managing that interface and navigating that natural tension. As a group, we have the potential to achieve something that we never could as a single organisation, and the impact we're already starting to have at the United Nations and other forums can be an incredibly powerful thing.

What are the things that keep you up at night?
Over the last 12 months plastics have almost become a four-letter word. Probably 60 per cent of my packaging is in plastics. According to

analysis, glass actually has a larger carbon footprint than plastics, but it is seen in a different light. Part of it is balancing our PR with real, underlying sustainability objectives. Ideally, we'd be ahead of public sentiment, where it's moving and what customers expect. Sometimes we're a little bit behind and need to catch up. We look for a source of innovation that not only solves an environmental or a social issue but will also be a source of competitive advantage for us.

Who has made a really big impact on your career?
The founder of Aesop, Dennis Paphitis, has had a big impact on me. I learnt from him the importance of focus – thinking about the long term. Even when we were growing and we had cashflow issues, he would loathe to make short-term decisions that would help our cash balance but damage the brand or the relationship with the customer. You start with something that is pure and clean and over time it dilutes.

Then my father, a small businessperson. I learnt an incredible work ethic and a perspective that if you work hard enough at something, you can solve it. I never saw him give up. He was a great role model.

What gets you out of bed in the morning?
Seeing the incredible changes that are occurring in the industry in channels and thinking about how we're going to solve them. It feels like an unbelievably challenging moment and environment. On a daily basis, it's the people I work with, the brand that we deal with, and our stores.

Interview: DU, London

What separates people as careers progress is the soft skills – empathy, ability to influence people, to get on with different cultures.

You need to be bold in your vision, even if at first blush you can't figure out how to get there. What we've done is mapped out a direction and, over time, gradually started to fill in what the steps look like.

Matthew Crummack

POSITION AT TIME OF INTERVIEW:
CEO of GoCompare, consumer comparison site (UK-based)

Matthew Crummack is CEO of GoCompare and serves as a Non-Executive director at National Express.

Prior to that, Matthew was CEO of lastminute.com from 2011, and led it through its acquisition by lastminute.com Group (formerly known as Bravofly Rumbo Group) in March 2015. He previously held leadership roles at Expedia and Nestle, having started his career at Procter & Gamble (P&G).

Currently based in the UK, Matthew's work has taken him all over the world, including the US, Asia and the Middle East. As GoCompare looks to build traction for its innovative auto-switching service weflip, Matthew reflects on his career and what connects people to an organisation.

What initially drew you to the world of business?
I started reading quite early. I first asked my parents to subscribe to *The Economist* at the age of 16. Did I read every copy? No! Some remained in their plastic, but I was always interested. I remember watching the career of my father, an engineer. In the late 70s, his industry blew up, so I grew up listening to those stories. I wanted to know how economics and business played into that. Because of all this, I had quite a strong philosophy around wanting to get working as soon as I could, to take responsibility for myself. Financially, I couldn't do this as early as I would have liked, so I enjoyed university!

Was there ever any doubt about whether you would go to university?
It was a very different world for us. Both my grandfathers were coal miners and left school at 13. My father was the first person in his family to go to university. He always spoke about working hard and taking responsibility for yourself, so my siblings and I grew up with this idea that, if you apply yourself and work hard, you can achieve. I was interested in studying further but, after I'd finished university and tasted work experience during the summer, I wanted to get cracking.

Your father was clearly a role model. Have others been particularly influential for you?
Yes, there are a few people I have met over time. One of my early mentors was a senior executive at Procter & Gamble, John Millen. He was very principled, very driven, very straight in the way he did business – and very successful. Equally, Paul Polman, most recently at Unilever, was very driven and very principled. I really like working with people that. I learnt a lot from Dara Khosrowshahi, now CEO of Uber. He was a visionary leader. From West Coast, to very European, to very British, I've seen quite different styles over time. What I've found is that you will learn a lot from people who are very consistent in their principles and in how they deal with people.

From Expedia in the US, to P&G and lastminute.com with its big European footprint – and then the takeover – you must have worked with many leadership styles. Did you have to consciously adapt to leading in different cultures?
The training at P&G for eight or nine years was incredible but it was also a relatively protected environment. When I left, two experiences shaped me a lot. One was working with a company of 45 people, doing below-the-line marketing agency work. There weren't any departments helping you do things. *You* had to do stuff. It was a real awakening.

The second experience was moving to the US. I had worked in Europe a lot and had built a good understanding of the different things at play. I'd worked for an American business but moving to the US and managing US-based teams was totally different. I realised my style, communication and management were still very, very British – a little bit Hugh Grant in *Four Weddings and a Funeral*. In that environment, if you don't get to the point, you can quickly get stuck and outplayed. I had to adapt. Looking back, I don't think I could do what I do now if I hadn't gone through that.

Is there an environment that you feel suits you best?
Working in an organisation that is small enough to control and big enough to have scale, where you can make stuff happen, at pace – I enjoy that. Whether I would go back to a million-employee business, I don't know. It's very different from the one I'm at now. Here, it's a team of very talented people who I trust and have fun with but that can also make a lot happen.

Looking at your career, you've been here and there in terms of decisions. Was there a eureka moment, and how did you decide to move from P&G to Expedia?
When I moved from Nestle to Expedia, consumer goods at the time were called 'fast-moving'. Arriving at Expedia – a digital environment – I suddenly realised the pace at which companies could innovate and outcompete their rivals by simply changing their approach and business model. This was 'fast-moving'.

It presented a very different intellectual and operational challenge. One moment stands out. I was only a few weeks into the job at Expedia, in a conference room in Berlin, and I drew on the board a virtual schematic of our digital supply chain. It looked like a schematic of the actual supply chain from a physical goods manufacturer. It was the same thing! One has bytes of information moving around and the other has a case of physical goods. It's the same principle; it's just that things move in different ways. It was a revelatory moment - where you understand where you are now and decide to see how you can break down these different concepts into more manageable elements and figure out how to do it.

Of course, it's the power of visualising the value chain. You're right, lots of organisations are creating something, packaging it...
It's the same with the types of people you have in the business. You talk to engineers who believe they are the real engineers because they deal with machines. They are all straight talking and numbers-focused. You go to a bunch of software engineers and they are no different. They are very straight talking, and they just want to get on with the job with no fluff. There are similar themes; it's just that one's an engine and one's not. So, what you tend to find is that today's software industry is today's engineering world. There are just different problems.

Was it a big decision to leave P&G?
It was a little bit of a crazy move. I was doing well and had been promoted up the organisation. At the time of handing my notice in, my wife was due to have twins. I left P&G just as they were born, to go work for a 45-person SME based in Newcastle with a vision to reinvent the way below-the-line marketing was done. It was a massively naïve move. I was rose-tinted as to what was achievable there. Looking back though, I wouldn't do anything differently. I learnt a lot in a short space of time. But yes, it was a curious move.

Or courageous?
Courageous and downright maverick or stupid. People did look at me like I had three heads at the time and, looking back, I can see why.

Is there anything you particularly look for in people when it comes to skills, attitude and characteristics?
For me, attitude, self-awareness and drive trump knowledge and skill set. I've worked with people who are constantly reinventing themselves through experiences that make them want to do better; through self-drive, being a self-starter and being prepared to work together. We have all sorts of people on the team, with different backgrounds and skillsets and I think, again, it doesn't really matter where you've come from. It's about how you perform and how you take responsibility for situations.

In terms of attracting talent in the future, how do you think organisations can best learn and adapt to the changes we are seeing in what people are attracted to?
There is a desire in the demographic coming into the workforce now to work on 'ideas' and to work for businesses that are doing something unique or good. In the 90s, it was banking. Maybe there is a change.

However, there has always been a difference between those who are quite happy to work just for themselves and those for whom a salary is a by-product of something they really enjoy doing and want to get better at. Businesses will naturally have both these things as they scale. It needs to be an environment that creates trust, creates openness and is human, not soulless. Flexibility is important but, ultimately, I think people like working together in offices or in spaces where they can chat. People make friends and marry through work!

We are social animals ...
That's right. I don't think we will all be working from home, or in virtual pods. We're still going to have people who want to sit together and solve problems together.

We've talked about engineers as not typically being the type for the softer side of things, but you take community and culture quite seriously. How do you overcome the sometimes-understandable cynicism or reticence and demonstrate clear ROI?
The difference I've seen over the years is between those who have not bought in at all, those who've half-bought in and the people who are engaged and trying to do the best that they can. The difference can be a 20 to 30% increase in output with full engagement and, conversely, a 20 to 30% dilution if not engaged at all.

Being engaged is not simply turning up occasionally and presenting a corporate strategy of what you need to do. It's recognising you must give people time if you want them to connect what they do on PowerPoint to the feel of the business. Through repetition and consistency with people and by giving people the time for feedback, they generally buy in more and lose their cynicism.

Do some people get impatient with that?
It's difficult to know what the right pace is between people who just need a bit more time to adjust and those who will never adjust. There isn't a magic solution. What you can't do though is be held hostage to those who can't move on; you are either on the bus or you're not. But you need to at least give people time to adjust.

How do you get the confidence to make calls about which direction GoCompare should take and how do you manage any seeds of doubt?
I've never been one to try to optimise my way out of a situation incrementally. There are businesses around like that but, in the types of business I work in now, the world of technology is moving too fast to take a conservative view of change. You need to be bold in your vision, even if at first blush you can't figure out how to get there. What we've done is mapped out a direction and, over time, gradually started to fill in what the steps look like. Sometimes in the staircase there are little kinks, or a step missed out, and you climb down again. But, broadly, we have a pretty clear vision that people believe in, which enables us to keep going and learning on an everyday basis.

Are there particular moments you are most proud of in your career?
Yes, a couple. When I first started managing Pringles in the UK, we were playing against PepsiCo Europe who managed Walkers and were the world leader in snacking. We asked ourselves how we could compete against a giant. But we were able to convince UK retailers to put curved shelving into supermarkets – it gave the brand some focus

in store, and it really helped us compete. I still look back at it and think how that was quite a cool moment.

At lastminute.com, selling the brand and company lastminute.com (a going concern) to another business is something I'm proud of. It has retained jobs and the lastminute.com brand. Knowing the background and how unstraightforward it was, I feel good about that. There are numerous points in time, but sometimes it takes the benefit of hindsight for you to see the results.

Interview: AC, London

I don't think we will all be working from home, or in virtual pods. We're still going to have people who want to sit together and solve problems together.

Really think about how you are going to change people's lives. There are so many innovative and smart concepts emerging every day, so you really need to think: 'how do I make my proposition something that truly makes a difference?

Susanne Given

POSITION AT TIME OF INTERVIEW:
Chair of Made.com, digital retail (UK-based)

Before becoming Chair of Made.com in 2016, Susanne Given had already made a formidable mark on the retail sector. Her career spans the full length of the high street, with spells working for John Lewis, TK Maxx, Harrods and House of Fraser. From 2012 to 2015, Susanne was COO of SuperGroup Plc. We interviewed Susanne in 2017, and were keen to understand her leadership style, get under the skin of the challenges facing the retail sector, and find out how she uses her traditional corporate experience to help digital start-ups.

Since our interview, Susanne has taken up the position of Non-Executive Chairman at both Push Doctor and Outfittery. She also is a Non-Executive Director at Eurostar International, Titraz BB Reit Plc, Al Tayer Group and at Deloitte NSE LLP.

Whilst we were getting ready for this interview, you mentioned how important a role model your mother has been. What have you learned from her?
I grew up with two sisters who suffered from extreme Autism and, to this day, my mother has dedicated her entire life to the care of them both. She taught me what it looks like to be dedicated, caring and compassionate towards those who are less fortunate in life.

You mother sounds like an amazing role model. Throughout your career, have there been people who have influenced you professionally?
If I go back to the early stages of my career, the two co-founders of Furniture Village, David Imrie and Peter Harrison, gave me a great opportunity to step into a role that exceeded my previous experience, all at a time when the business was growing rapidly. This gave me the opportunity to step-up and shine, and they were very much instrumental in nurturing my move into retail.

Further downstream, I joined Harrods in 2001, just as Marty Wikstrom had joined the business as the new MD. She was a formidable female executive and really supported and sponsored female talent; her encouragement of other female executives stands out as a distinct moment that made me realise the level of sponsorship required for women in business. Growing up in Scandinavia, I wasn't familiar with the level of gendered hierarchy that was apparent in the UK at the time, and so watching Marty make sure these issues were addressed was a distinct moment of realisation.

Later in my career, Paul Sweetman of TJ Europe, an amazing retailer and successful executive at TJX, asked me to be MD at a point in time when I certainly didn't think it was credible. He kept pushing me and outlining that firstly, my peers were sponsors of the decision and that secondly, he wasn't terribly concerned about the external perspectives as he felt that I was the right person for the job. He was a real role model for how to invest in someone who perhaps wasn't the finished article.

How would you describe your leadership style?
I'm very direct and set out a clear path and vision for the teams that I work with. Whenever I go into a new team, I spend the first bit of time deeply immersed within the group to understand their capabilities and ambitions. Following that, I like to foster the right dynamic, getting individuals into senior leadership positions to create a high-quality team that can deliver, whatever the opportunity or challenge. I am also a very supportive executive, so I spend a significant amount of time with people who are feeling stretched in their roles. Having benefited from similar support in the past, I think it's important to pass that on.

Looking back, what has been your greatest business achievement *so far?*

You're making me pick one? It's between TJX and Supergroup (now Superdry). At TJX, it was a special achievement to take over from a larger than life, successful character and continue to run the business during a period of very fast expansion, whilst at the same time delivering the highest level of profitability that the division had ever achieved. In terms of the most challenging, turning Supergroup around will definitely go down as the toughest opportunity I've ever stepped into. When I joined Supergroup the share price had collapsed; turning that business around from an operational and business strategy point of view, while also regaining investor confidence, was unbelievably tough.

What do you see as the key challenges in the world of retail, specifically fashion retailers, over the next 2-3 years?

I would frame the next 2-3 years in the context of 2023 being just around the corner. In 2023, 50% of the consumer base will be millennials or younger, a seismic shift for an industry that's already gone through a lot of change over the past decade. The biggest challenge over this time frame will be to face-up to these kinds of shifts by taking the time to truly understand what they will mean.

Another substantial challenge is that we have a lot of fantastic boards around the country, however, these boards are made up of individuals with experience within a consumer era that's drawing to a close. Unless changes are made to the general composition of boards over the next 2-3 years, they and their businesses are going to find it very difficult to confront digital change.

Do you think there is too much emphasis on big data?

I don't think there's too much emphasis on big data, but rather there is too little emphasis placed on converting it into something meaningful. Because business leaders face so many different streams of activity when moving businesses into the digital era … it means that utilising data in an intelligent manner is up against a lot of competing priorities.

Do you think that there is a bright future for the physical retail store?

Yes, I do. However, I think there will be considerably fewer stores and that they will become a space in which you experience a brand to decide if it's right for you. If you go back 15 years, somebody who was in their mid-20s or 30s would have looked forward to spending their weekends going out to search through stores. People don't do that anymore – that's a habit which has gone. Now before they buy, customers want to be convinced that you are a great business, a great retailer and a great brand. I think the physical store will evolve to be about brand experiences rather than more passive weekend browsing.

You have quite a portfolio career now, and that is something you have done by design; what is the best thing for you about this sort of career?

I set out on a portfolio career about 12 months ago and wanted to split my portfolio 50:50 between early stage digital business and maintaining a foot in my old world of corporate, larger-scale operations. I decided that the early stage digital space would be a crucial opportunity to stay current over coming years. The opportunity to get involved with a business like Outfittery, who is at the cutting edge of the personalised men's shopping experience, is phenomenal.

In my view, it's incredibly important to invest your time in business with a view to be continually learning. There are two reasons for this: firstly, you keep yourself fresh; secondly, you are offering those businesses your experience of how you scale and manage resources, something which can be tough to manage. From a corporate point of view, the learning that you take from an early stage digital business can offer a perspective of what digital change actually looks like. If you've built your portfolio in the right way, you can cross-pollinate between the two, building up and applying relevant expertise to either type of business.

What advice would you give to Gen Zs starting out in business today?

Really think about how you are going to change people's lives. There are so many innovative and smart concepts emerging every day, so you really need to think: 'how do I make my proposition something that truly makes a difference?' Whenever I sit down with early stage businesses, that is the first question I ask them. It's very interesting because it really distinguishes the people who have a clear vision around their concept, business and brand from those who don't.

Last year you climbed Kilimanjaro to raise funds for charity, what made you decide that this is something you wanted to do and why did you do it?

I had been very ill the year before, I was in hospital for a long time and had an extended recuperation period of 3 months. It is a very sobering moment when you suddenly feel you own mortality. Once I got back on my feet, a dear friend of mine, who has battled breast cancer for a decade, asked me if I would come and climb with her on behalf of the charity Breast Cancer Now.

I decided it served two purposes: one, my grandmother died of breast cancer; and two, it felt like a great way to mark the anniversary of a personal life-threatening situation. I'm actually planning on climbing Kilimanjaro once again next year for a child bereavement charity after attempting to climb Mont Blanc this year.

Physical and mental fitness is obviously an important part of how you live your life, is that something you demand of the people around you?
I don't demand it, but I would say I encourage it. Again, talking about this 2023 switch, that's what millennials will build into their lives and so we should all try to do the same. Ultimately, it will become part of the way everyone lives.

Interview: OP, London

Always put the business first.

Alex Gourlay

POSITION AT TIME OF INTERVIEW:
Co-Chief Operating Officer for Walgreens Boots Alliance, Inc. (US-based)

Having worked with Boots since the 1970s, in everything from Health & Beauty to Boots the Chemists, Alex Gourlay is something of a company veteran. It is this breadth of experience within the company, Alex tells us, that has helped to keep him grounded: 'You should never let ego or rank get in the way because the health of the business depends on it.' We interviewed Alex in 2012 when Alex was Chief Executive of Health & Beauty of Alliance Boots, shortly after the US retailer Walgreens bought a 45% stake in Boots. He talks about the 'stickability' of Boots, what he sees for its future, and reviving the high street.

Alex, you've been part of the Boots world for many years. What has been its 'stickability' for you?
I like working for a healthcare company but also in a more commercial, business-oriented environment than the public sector like the NHS. Working for Boots offers an attractive mix of competitiveness and care.

A lot of change is to be expected over the next few years, as a result of Boots' partnership Walgreens. How will you be engaging your people through the change process?
Firstly, both Boots and Walgreens are healthcare companies and therefore culturally similar so we will make sure that we engage people in the history of both companies. Secondly, there will be a combination of rational and emotional engagement.

On a rational level, each company makes money in different places. Boots makes money from wholesaling, retail and manufacturing amongst other areas whereas Walgreens focuses on pharmacy and practicing as well as retail. So, there are certain areas to share without overlapping.

In terms of the big picture, the UK is an important market but there will be expansion from the UK to the global market. It will be an ambitious project for everyone so there will also be an emotional angle to engagement, as we will need to engage people quickly. This is already happening; in fact, two members of HR on the Boots UK Work Inspiration Programme recently picked up an Inspiration Award and were able to answer questions on recent events at Boots because they were fully engaged.

One of the things we have seen at another British brand, Burberry, albeit it a very different one to Boots, is how they moved from being a very UK-focused business to one that has exported Britishness to new markets. They have utilised employee mobility across the different geographies they're now operating in. Is employee mobility one of the things that you hope will happen between Boots and Walgreens in the years to come?
Burberry is a global brand, but Boots is a global platform that is also applied locally. Being community-based is one of Boots' strengths, indicated by its community pharmacy.

So, departments that will exist on a global scale like HR and marketing will still deliver business locally to the marketplace.

What does being a good 'multi-channel retailer' mean for Boots?
The channels we use to get the product to market must ultimately be customer-led so our mindset must be customer0focused. We must move with the customer as they access new products and services.

The Boots Advantage Card is one of the best-known loyalty programmes in the UK. Is this the heartbeat of your multi-channel operation?

The Advantage Card is incredibly powerful and delivers key insight about our customers. It is an important part of our operation. That said, a lot of functions play very prominent roles in helping us deliver across different channels, including IT and, of course, those teams that work across the supply chain.

Boots has a presence on nearly every high street. If you could wave a magic wand, how would you go about reviving the high street?

The majority of customers want to be proud of their high street and their local community. People recognise that the high street suffers from high rents, excessive business rates and expensive parking. This makes it hard for trade to happen because it is uneconomic for both the customer and trader. We need to establish a cheaper model for the high street with lower business rates and lower costs for the consumer. Another thing that's really important to customers is the convenience of the high street, so partnerships and providing different services at different times are the way forward. Regarding the future of the high street, I believe two types will emerge. One will have a strong fashion base and the other will be based around daily food shopping, so it will be important to get local traders back on the high street. We need to redefine the high street and use the resources provided because people want it.

Who has been the biggest influence on your career?

I've worked with some amazing people and could name half a dozen who have really encouraged me. One incredibly influential person in recent years has been Stefano Pessina [the Executive Chairman at Walgreens Boots Alliance]. I really value his advice, respect his insight and admire his energy. I suppose at the end of the day the support from my father, my wife and my children has been the most important thing of all.

And finally, do you have a personal business motto?

Always put the business first. There can be a level of self-centredness with CEOs and I have learnt through business that people behave differently the more important they become. You should never let ego or rank get in the way because the health of the business depends on it.

Interview: OP, Nottingham

Feelings of doubt, fear, apathy come to everyone at different times – successful leaders continue to strive and overcome no matter what they feel. I believe the power of being someone of character and who can self-regulate their emotions will increasingly become a differentiating factor for future leaders.

Henry Ruiz

POSITION AT TIME OF INTERVIEW:
CEO of REA Group – Asia and Chief Strategy Officer.
Digital Media Sector (Australia-based)

Henry Ruiz is one of the movers and shakers at REA Group, based in Melbourne. He is a deeply experienced 'digital' operator and has been at the centre of digital commerce in Australia for the last twenty years or so.

REA Group is a digital media business with more than 1,500 people working across three continents to change the way the world experiences property. REA operates Australia's leading residential, commercial and share property websites – realestate.com.au, realcommercial.com.au, Flatmates.com.au – as well as Spacely, a short-term commercial and co-working property site.

Henry joined REA in 2009 initially as its Chief Product Officer, leading the teams responsible for creating property experiences for consumers and customers, before becoming the Chief Digital Officer in 2014.

In our interview with Henry, his passion for digital technology comes across keenly, as does his interest in consumer behaviour. It comes as no surprise to hear that he studied Psychology before pursuing a career in business.

What initially attracted you to the digital sector?
I was naturally curious when the internet started. I was just finishing my professional training as a psychologist and found myself messing around on this thing called 'the world-wide-web'. I received a phone call from a high school friend out of the blue. She asked me about human-computer interaction and wondered if I might be able to help out in an 'internet company'. Being the adventurous person that I am I said, "I probably can't .... but I'm happy to come over and have a chat!" And that's how I started my digital career. I learnt on the job about how to conduct usability testing on very early-stage websites.

You've been at REA for some time. What attracted you in the first place?
Yes, I have! It's been more that 10 years now. I think I had an inherent interest because REA was a digital pure play business and I saw a lot of opportunity for where the business was at the time, but also for what it could be. I deeply respected the CEO and I thought I could have meaningful input, not just in business strategy, but in developing future leaders.

How would you describe your personal and professional journey? And what's kept you at REA?

The ride has been amazing, I'm really thankful for the opportunities I've had. There are a couple of reasons I've loved being part of the REA journey for so long.

Firstly, what we do impacts people in such a meaningful way. Digital skills are in high demand. You can work for lots of different types of companies; some sectors add to people's lives, whilst others are less productive. Our space … it's a very meaningful part of life. The 'home' can be a place where people feel safe and nurtured.

Secondly, I am in awe of the teams we've built over time. You spend a lot of time at work. Having the ability to somewhat shape who you spend time with and learn from, inspires you and gives you energy. I believe this makes you a better human being.

There's a great working environment here – is attrition relatively low at REA as a result? Do people tend to stay and grow with the business?
Yes, we've had a lot of people who have not only stayed; they've grown with the business, which is really amazing. Every company has its own "magic", but I think one of the unique things at REA is people's openness and transparency. If you want to learn about any part of the business, to make you better in the context of your role, there isn't a person who wouldn't

sit down and spend time with you to explain how their role or function works. Learning on the job is a reality here.

So that's the DNA of this organisation, a very open culture?
Yes, it is. An open learning culture.

When leading a digital organisation like this, how do you ensure that your work remains agile and innovative across different regions?

The psychological jargon would be to 'have a growth mindset', but this is something that is very important to us. If you consider the digital landscape, the reality is that I don't think anybody can 100% accurately predict where it's going to end up. An openness to seeing different opportunities from where you are today is something that people aren't naturally wired to be comfortable with; it's not for everyone. What has held us in good stead is (1) being open and curious, (2) not assuming that we always know what the answer is, and (3) really focusing on who our customers and consumers are, and what their preferences and drivers are in relation to the property sector.

How do you see the market in Asia changing over the next few years?
Culturally the markets are very different, macro-economically they're different, and they're at a different phase in almost every dimension as it relates to property. Fundamentally, people want to find a property that matches their needs and use a trustworthy source of information that gives them a comprehensive and accurate view of the marketplace; this is a clear opportunity for us and it's the path that we're on. That said – transparency of property information is a challenge in some markets across SE Asia; so the credibility and reliability of real estate professionals is key to how those markets work.

How does the digital journey in Asia compare to Australia? Is it more or less advanced?
I would say it's both. It's more advanced in the sense that you have clearly got some major players coming out of China and SE Asia that are, on key metrics – whether it be audience or revenue – very sophisticated digital businesses. However, when you think about the property sector, it certainly hasn't progressed as much as some other marketplaces and that is where we are having a real impact.

If I contrast the REA journey 10 years ago, which was largely orientated around a large screen experience, mobile has certainly taken over since then. Our plans in Asia centre on small screen experiences and extend into large screen opportunities in the context of property.

Has your background in psychology helped you and the business?
In so many unforeseen ways! My advice to people going through university and thinking about postgraduate study is to do at least a semester of psychology, sociology or anthropology; anything that gets you to think about people. At the end of the day, business is about two people connecting and having a value exchange. I think it's very tempting to get all academic or 'ivory tower' about business but, ultimately, if you treat people well and value is created, monetisation and revenue can fall off the back of that. Anything that encourages people *to understand* others more deeply is a good thing to my mind.

You talk about two people connecting... that's deeply personalised. Is that a core philosophy for your business?
Yes. I think our focus on not thinking about our consumers or customers as a large collective group of people, but as individuals with differences in preferences, has made us more personalised in how we approach our overall strategy. This also helps us continuously guide the direction of the business to our true north and directly impacts the products that we build.

REA is a modern, digital business. Based on your experiences here, and what you see in other digital businesses, what are the traits of a successful "21st century" organisation?
I think it's the notion that everybody inside the business should be as informed as anyone else. Unless there are highly confidential matters that are market sensitive, we fundamentally believe in sharing as much context as possible. I think that's what gives us a competitive advantage. One of the biggest barriers for a 21st century business is the age-old issue of silos that happen inside companies. Therefore, your ability to build trust and a sense of community inside a business, while it can sound soft and fluffy, can truly give you a competitive edge.

In terms of silos and hierarchy, a lot of people talk about 'holacracy' being a mode that is important to 21st century organisations – is that the case here?
We certainly have levels of reporting lines and teams, but the word hierarchy feels foreign within the context of REA. There's a lot of meritocracy that we use, and ideas should come from anywhere. You could talk to our CEO or a developer and, if you didn't ask them what they do, you wouldn't know what their role is. I think there is a 'human-ness' and keeping it real in how we want people to act and lead in the company.

Being market-orientated means, we are more focused on the outside world than the inside. You have some companies that talk about being product or tech-led. I don't believe it's one or the other. We do all we can to be market-led. We use the analogy of the three-legged stool. You need to get the right technology, product and people working well to ultimately achieve a better outcome for your business.

What are the attributes and traits required of a 21st century CEO?

Humility, I think, more than anything else – but **genuine** humility, not fake humility like a humble-brag approach. When talking about authentic leadership, you can use all the buzz words like 'servant leadership' and 'the shadow of a leader', which are all important, but more than anything else you need someone who connects with their teams. When you've got real connection amongst your leadership team as well as other people you interact with in the business, people will follow you because you're bringing out the best in them as well as providing a safe space for people to grow and develop. Part of learning is making mistakes and people need to feel safe in doing this. Having a forgiving spirit and showing grace isn't something that's talked about much in business literature; and I think that's a missed opportunity. Businesses re-imagining marketplaces won't necessarily get everything right; and building the muscle of courage in your people is, in part, a reflection of leaders demonstrating humility and grace.

Who would you say have been the biggest influences on your career to date and what have you learnt from them?

I'd say my father was the biggest influence on me. He was a highly educated individual, a very accomplished chess player and had the typical immigration story to Australia. He was originally from Cuba. He ended his career working as a high school teacher. One of the things that he instilled in me is that there isn't anything you *can't* learn. This has really guided my life in many ways. As a student, it gave me confidence to learn new things, like the Internet, even though that wasn't my initial training. On the flip side, once I had my first leadership role, he'd remind me that "there are no bad students, just bad teachers". If my team doesn't understand me it's actually my responsibility to change my approach. It's my job to create the environment and the culture that allows them to flourish.

Did you ever beat your father at chess?

Ha. I thought I had. When I was about 10, my Uncle visited. He was also accomplished at chess having won some championships back in the US. He and my dad played a match he managed to win. Later that day, I challenged my uncle to a match and won! I thought, "Right, I've got my dad covered." It went to my head a bit, for about 24 hours to exact; until he sat me down and demolished me. I was genuinely shocked. Little did I realise that my dad had also let my Uncle win.

Is there anyone professionally that has influenced you?

There are too many people to single people out – anyone I've worked closely with over my career has influenced me. I've taken so many things from them, whether it's back in my counselling days as a psychologist, my early internet years, or my experience working for and seeing 4 amazing & diverse CEOs in action. I've also learnt a lot from exposure to the REA board over the last decade and the executive teams I have worked with over that time. Everyone brings different things to the table. They've helped, shaped and refined me, hopefully for the better.

What are you most proud of?

Without question, my family and particularly my children. I'm proud of the fact they are doing the best they can to honour the opportunity that my parents gave me in migrating to Australia. Clearly biasedly, I think our kids are turning into good human beings with good hearts.

What advice would you give to a Generation Z-er starting out in business today?

I'd say a couple of things. Always keep checking that you have an open mindset to learning new things. Make the most of every opportunity, wherever you are. Don't be in a rush – play the long game. Wherever you are; be present. And, more than anything else, develop your belief in yourself and how you lead others. Feelings of doubt, fear, apathy come to everyone at different times – successful leaders continue to strive and overcome no matter what they feel. I believe the power of being someone of character and who can self-regulate their emotions will increasingly become a differentiating factor for future leaders.

Interview: OP, Melbourne

Wherever you are, be present.

'Our worst fears, like our greatest hopes, are not outside our powers, and we can come in the end to triumph over the former and to achieve the latter.'

— Marcel Proust, *In Search of Lost Time*

Riccardo Zacconi
Simon Gillespie, OBE
Natalie Acton and Ella Joseph
Helen Nash
Jonathan Powell
Olly Olsen
Alison Loehnis
Olayinka Aresa
Tony Danker

QUARTER FOUR

2018–2020 In Search of Lost Time

TRUMP SWIPES
THE NEXT BRITISH PM......
GREAT HAIR!!!
HILARY CLINTON
SADIQ KHAN
A MEXICAN
NO
NO
NO
NO
NO
NO
NO
NO
tinder
BORIS

Delivering Brexit, or stopping it, had become a national obsession in the UK by now. After a period of 'waiting and seeing' businesses decided they couldn't hold on forever, and began making plans again irrespective of if/when/how Brexit was delivered. We talk Brexit, and other things, with Jonathan Powell (CEO of Inter Mediate), one of the most successful negotiators of the last 25 years, widely acclaimed for his role in the Northern Ireland Peace Process.

As Q5 grew, the work and clients, became more diverse. Which is reflected in our last batch of interviewees. Despite leading very different organisations, both Riccardo Zacconi (CEO and co-founder of King) and Simon Gillespie (CEO of the British Heart Foundation) tell us the importance of attracting and retaining the best talent globally now and in the future.

By the start of 2019, mental health was fiercely on our agenda. An independent review of the Mental Health Act took place in 2018, and numerous campaigns brought the topic front of mind. Natalie Acton and Ella Joseph, co-CEOs of Think Ahead, a fast-track mental health social work graduate scheme, talk about how they have made the organisation, and their CEO job-share, a success.

In 2018 we launched the Q5 youth panel with fourteen 16 to 17-year-olds. The future workforce, Generation Z, is characterised by strong ideals and a sense of purpose. For them a company whose purpose you believe in is the single most important driver when choosing a career and employer. It's a common theme across our interviews with Yinka Aresa (a member of our first Youth Panel), Helen Nash (CEO of Metcash), Alison Loehnis (the President of Net-a-Porter and Mr Porter) and Olly Olsen (co-CEO of The Office Group). All stress the importance of purpose and passion in their work.

We end with Tony Danker (Incoming Director General of the CBI), the only interview that took place since the COVID-19 pandemic. Tony gives his views on the leadership lessons from this crisis, and what it means for the next generation entering the workforce.

Being a leader is about encouraging discussion, as much as it is about making decisions.

Riccardo Zacconi

POSITION AT TIME OF INTERVIEW:
Co-Founder and CEO of King, maker of Candy Crush.
Gaming Industry (UK-based)

Riccardo was born in Rome. He gained a Bachelor's degree in economics from the Libera Università Internazionale degli Studi Sociali Guido Carli, before embarking on the early part of his career in consulting. However, Riccardo is probably best known as one of the founders of King, the gaming company.

We interviewed Riccardo Zacconi back in 2017 when he was CEO of King. After more than 16 years at the helm of the global entertainment business, he stepped down in early 2019. The company made its name with the development of Candy Crush, one of the most profitable apps ever invented.

At the time of our interview in 2017, the company had over 300 million monthly active users and, in 2018, net revenues of $2.1 billion. But it wasn't always smooth sailing: 2009 was King's 'most difficult lesson', Riccardo observes, 'when our industry was disrupted very quickly by Facebook'. In this interview, we ask Riccardo about overcoming obstacles like these, his career choices, and his advice for 'Generation Z'.

How would you describe your leadership style?

To be a good leader, you have to listen, be ambitious, and challenge beyond the obvious. You also have to be able to think two steps ahead. We have a team-orientated culture at King. Being a leader is about encouraging discussion, as much as it is about making decisions. We're all rational people; if there are different views then there must be different assumptions about what we're trying to achieve. This is where discussion needs to happen … not just a decision. Also, I always try to make sure I hire people better than me, and then give them autonomy. The best measure of a leader is how good the team is they've put together.

How has your leadership role evolved through the history of King – from being a private company through the IPO, to becoming an independent subsidiary of Activision Blizzard?

When we first started, we did everything ourselves. Most of my time was focused on ensuring all the work in my area was done. Once we expanded a bit, the next stage was to actively manage people. But even then, I would still be involved in the detail, and made most of the decisions. Finally, you reach the stage when you're large enough to bring in 'managers'. You need to hire the best, and then give them the space to manage people and make decisions. Your role is now to provide challenge, to ensure we're being ambitious enough and thinking far enough into the future.

Looking back over your career – who has been the major influencer on your career?

My team. They give continuous feedback. One piece of feedback I've been reflecting on recently, is that as leaders, we feel we should always sweep in and add some value. But sometimes that value-add might only be 5%, and in the process of giving it, we've taken away 80% of motivation. At times, I've learnt that it's best not to intervene.

It has been an incredible journey for King over the last ten years or so. What have been your most painful lessons?

The most difficult lesson we went through was during 2009, when our industry was disrupted very quickly by Facebook. We had partnered with Yahoo, which was the largest portal on the web, and in that one year from May 2009 to May 2010 Yahoo Games lost 45% of their users. We knew we had to crack Facebook, but it wasn't easy. It took us until April 2011 before we launched our first game on Facebook. Managing a company in growth is easy, but managing a company that needs to transition is much more difficult. You have to manage your investors, your board and, of course, your team. The most important thing I learnt during this time was to be 100% open. It's important to tell the people around you, your investors … how things really are. I remember saying, 'We need to crack Facebook. If we don't, we'll cease to exist!'

So how did you achieve this in practical terms?

We split our organisation into two parts; one part focused on the existing business, to make sure we had a lifeline. This meant maintaining as many users as possible ... so that we could, ultimately, pay the bills. The other half of the company was focused entirely on cracking Facebook. The whole team demonstrated fantastic teamwork and humility. A lot of people wanted to focus on making new games, but couldn't, as we had to focus on maintaining our position. We achieved the right balance.

It's clear that the culture of King is incredibly important. How have you managed to maintain your culture when you've grown as fast as you have?

Culture is created from the top. People entering the company look to people already there to see how they should behave. It's important to be a vulnerable leader - someone who people feel they can talk openly to, and someone who is open to criticism. People also need to feel comfortable with disagreeing with the leader and suggesting alternative ideas. Everyone in the team needs to feel shared ownership, both so that they feel valued, but also so that they are pulling in the same direction. You can have a boat with the best engine in the world – yet none of that matters if there's a hole in the bottom – it's still going to sink.

How does London stack up globally as a city to attract entrepreneurial and digital companies?

London is one of the key locations for start-ups in the world, and that is part because of the history behind it. Historically, London has been the binding element between the US and Europe. When American companies decide where to build their base for Europe, they usually start it in London, and quite simply that is because of language. This has helped create a large ecosystem of tech companies, as well as investors, many of whom came over from the US. Furthermore, the UK has created a place where both human talent and start-ups nurtured. We must be very careful to maintain and develop this.

Do you think that's particularly true in light of Article 50 being triggered?

Yes, absolutely. Top of the list when deciding this deal to leave the EU must be ensuring talent from all around the world is encouraged to come here, and that talent already here gets confirmation that they can stay.

You must have a huge number of international employees in this business?

We have employees of 71 different nationalities in London alone. We have 600 people here, and 40% of them are non-British. The best tech people in the world – from the US, from Sweden, from many places – we bring them to London. Some of those people stay with us, but others leave King and set up their own businesses and continue to create jobs and wealth for London and the UK.

It's obviously an incredibly competitive marketplace you're in, so what are some of the levers you use to attract top tech talent to your business?
Well it's obviously a lot easier now than 13 years ago when we were insignificant and had no users. We now have a number of things that attract top people. Firstly, we have more users than the population of the USA, so when we create a great game, we can show it to the world. Secondly, we are very profitable, so we can invest a lot on marketing, which allows even more people to learn about us. Thirdly, we have amazing people – the best in their field. This is certainly my motivation to come to work every day – to work with these people. Fourthly, we have a very flat hierarchy, where we try our best to empower people and give them responsibility.

What would be your advice to the new crop of talent that are leaving university now – the Generation Z?
The advice I would give isn't specific to any one generation. The first thing is to do something where you can learn as much as possible; to do this you need to go where the best people are. You learn so much more from people than you do from books. Secondly, it's often difficult to know what you want, but it's usually easier to know what you don't want. When I started, I knew I wanted to build my own company, but I didn't know what it would be or how I would get there. So, to start out with I decided not to do specific things, which meant that I tended to choose things which were of a more generalist nature, like working in consulting, which still allowed me to keep my options open.

It's not such a bad career consulting, is it?
Not at all. For me I always knew I wanted to end up doing something else, and consulting allowed me to learn things and gain experience without closing doors. The other thing you need, especially when becoming an entrepreneur, is patience. Any time you start a company, you place all your eggs in one basket. So, you want to make sure you have the right people to do it with, the right experience, and the right idea.

Do you have a personal motto that you live and work by?
I don't have motto for work, but I do have a personal belief for life in general and how to achieve happiness. I don't believe that happiness is a status, rather a variation of a status. For example, a Russian oligarch who dines on caviar every day can be far less happy than a person on the street who hasn't eaten for days, but suddenly has a burger. So, wherever you are in life, you have to look for improvements, and no matter what level you're starting at, improvement can still bring you happiness. The more you have, the harder it is to improve, so I see failure and down-turns as creating more opportunity for future improvements. This is life. When you're up, you must be careful; and when you're down, you must be hopeful.

Interview: OP, London

The best measure of a leader is how good the team is they've put together.

You need to be able to provide stability but there also need to be the agility to respond to circumstances.

Simon Gillespie, OBE

POSITION AT TIME OF INTERVIEW:
CEO of British Heart Foundation. Charity Sector (UK-based)

When we interviewed Simon Gillespie, he was the CEO of the British Heart Foundation (BHF). He had previously spent seven years being the CEO of the Multiple Sclerosis (MS) Society.

Simon's early career was in the Royal Navy, including command of HMS Sheffield and advising government ministers. From 2000 to 2004, he was Director of Operations at the Charity Commission. He then moved to become Head of Operations at the Healthcare Commission. In this interview, Simon talks about his career and how charities need to constantly keep pace with changing trends and behaviours in order to be successful.

Simon was awarded an OBE in 2019 by Her Majesty Queen Elizabeth II in her Birthday Honours, and recently retired from his CEO role at the BHF.

What did you do before joining the BHF?
I started off in the Royal Navy and was with them for 23 years. After I was medically discharged in 2000, I had to find myself something else to do, so I went to the Charity Commission as Director of Operations. From there, I was part of a start-up team for the Healthcare Commission. After that, I went on to become CEO of the Multiple Sclerosis Society before joining the BHF about six years ago.

If you consider the challenges you've experienced since joining the BHF, which did you expect, and which came as a surprise?
I think I was quite surprised at how underplayed the BHF was in terms of matching up their great reputation with their fundraising effort. There are about three times as many people with heart circulatory disease in the UK than there are cancer survivors, yet the cancer charities find it a lot easier to get money in. It was surprising for me to find that an organisation with such a big reputation was backed up with a significantly lower propensity to give than, for example, the cancer charities.

Has the propensity to give to an organisation like the BHF shifted over time?
Yes, it's slow to move but we always knew this. We're an ambitious organisation, currently investing in more than half of the UK's investment in circulatory disease research. We want the UK to do more in terms of getting the money in, for us to fund the lifesaving research that we do.

What have been the leadership challenges you've experienced?
The key thing for me relates to developing our team. In the case of the BHF, that's 4,200 paid staff and 20,000 volunteers. You need to start with the kernel of that: who the leaders are in the organisation; how they're organised; and how their departments and responsibilities are arranged in order to deliver the best possible outcomes. The BHF is still a pretty traditional organisation but we have made some major steps forward in exciting areas around technology, not just in terms of funding research but also in developing our in-house skills and expertise so that we enhance our capability and capacity to become more efficient and effective.

How far along the spectrum of volunteer-based delivery to professional delivery do you think there is still to go?
There's a long way. The key thing is recognising that there isn't a one-size-fits-all model. You need to be the right size, shape and culture of organisation for the issue that you're dealing with. It wouldn't be appropriate to think that an organisation solely comprised of volunteers

could organise a research programme of £100 million a year. We wouldn't dream of saying that we represent every single person in the UK with circulatory heart disease but what we do is organise ourselves to deliver the best possible research programme that we can and take the first steps in bringing that research into action for the benefit of patients.

There's got to be a mixed market. Public perception is interesting; there's a perception that there shouldn't be anyone paid in the charity sector. This comes back to the not 'one-size-fits-all' issue. If your organisation is primarily expertise-led, then you have to be led by that expertise, which doesn't come for free. If you've got the type of organisation that is looking for longer-term, sustainable global impact, your researchers have got to be able to rely on the fact that there will be money there to fund the next steps of their research. Maintaining momentum around research is important. After the last recession, the BHF decided it would limit its research investment quite significantly and it's taken a long time since then to regenerate that research capacity and interest in heart circulatory disease.

What's your perspective on the shift to e-commerce and how are you addressing it?

We've been remarkably adaptive in the 30 to 35 years that we've been involved in charity retail. Even though we weren't the first charity to enter into the retail market, we've developed into the biggest charity retailer chain in the country. We are very heavily reliant on our more than 735 shops and stores across the country, including our 175 furniture & electrical stores which generate half of our revenue. We have also seen a growth in our eBay presence, which started off about 10 years ago when we saw an opportunity to take advantage of high-value items that were being donated. That's grown from two guys doing it as a hobby, to a light industrial warehouse in Leeds employing over 60 people. It will turn over £6 million this year.

What have been the ingredients for your success in the charity retail market?

To an extent, I was talking about this earlier in terms of the mix between paid staff and volunteers. We've very clearly taken the view that you need to provide a good core of paid staff in the shops and stores to ensure proper management. This also means that the other staff and volunteers feel supported. We've placed an emphasis on professional retail management. We watch it very carefully to make sure the mix is right and it's important to keep fine-tuning this in terms of staffing and volunteers. It's a never-ending balancing act.

How has the nature of your volunteers changed over time, and have you needed to be clearer about what you offer people?
There's undoubtedly been a change, and the nature of our volunteers will always be changing. There are still a large number of retirees who volunteer in our shops but what we have seen is an increasing number of young people coming through. Sometimes that's through the Duke of Edinburgh (DofE) scheme. Sometimes it's people who want to get back into the job market after a career break, for whom the opportunity to volunteer with us provides a structured programme. We've had to shift our offer over the last 10 years to make sure we're offering enough flexibility to attract people. It's also important that we offer a social experience for people and a nice environment, not just in terms of the physicality of it but actually liking the people you're working with.

Fundamental to all of this is that our shop and store managers, assistant managers and regional staff must understand volunteers' motivations and what we need to offer to them. For instance, with DofE we ensure there's an environment where managers understand what the aim of the DofE scheme is and try to make sure that someone who is volunteering primarily to tick boxes is getting something else in addition to that.

What do you think Brexit means for the charity sector?
I'll start off with what I think it means for BHF. Our view hasn't changed since the run up to the referendum campaign; Brexit fundamentally affects three things. The first is an obvious point about people and the free movement of people in research and clinical environments. About 30 per cent of BHF funded researchers and research team members come from non-UK/EU countries. Anything that makes people more likely to leave the UK and return home, or less likely to come to the UK in the first place, is ultimately a detriment to the research environment here as well as to the NHS. Free movement is also fundamentally important in terms of developing researchers. People from the UK often need to go abroad to broaden their experience, develop new skills and learn new techniques. Any inhibition to this is concerning.

The second point is about money. The UK is a beneficiary of UK research funds, i.e., we get out more money than we pay in. This is significant in underpinning a lot of the excellent research facilities we have here. If it becomes more difficult for UK institutions to join those collaborative ventures or bids for money, it means they'll be looking for sources of income from other places, which is likely to put more strain on domestic funding sources like the BHF.

The final point is about regulation. In the UK we benefit from unified regulation across Europe in areas like clinical trials, medicines and healthcare products. The UK becomes a far less attractive environment to try new products if there's a bigger market across the channel. This means it's far more likely a manufacturer will get clearance in Europe first and then potentially come to the UK market later. This isn't black and white but what we will see over the next few years is new medicines being used in Europe before they're used in the UK, which is a big shift from a tradition that's been established for a century.

What is success for the BHF? If there is a destination, what does it look like?

There's a clear destination, which is that nobody should have the fear of heart circulatory disease. We'd like people with the disease to be diagnosed early enough to receive effective treatments that ensure it has minimum impact on their lives. That might be a 50- or 100-year view but what you must do within that is set yourself 5- to 10-year ambitions and be prepared to modify those as you go along. The key thing for us is about influencing. We are primarily a medical research funded charity, which gives us authority. We know a lot of things, so how can we use this knowledge, tie it together with who we are and our reputation to subsequently benefit people with heart circulatory disease as much as possible?

To what extent do you look to other organisations across the sector, learn from them and engage with them for mutual benefit?

Any good organisation will always be looking at what other people are doing, whether they're competitors or not. The charity sector is a very interesting mixture of competition and collaboration. We are always looking at who we would regard as our benchmarks in the charity and commercial sectors. To be successful in an increasingly volatile and unpredictable operating environment, organisations need to be looking for the right ideas. From my position as CEO, the issue is trying to look at where the market trends are. We need to ensure that we're not too far behind the curve. It's worth investing early to make sure we're making as much of a difference to people with heart circulatory disease as possible. The organisation itself has got to be constantly changing in order to deliver against the needs of the people.

Do you think the charity sector is well served by the model of having a board of trustees?

My view has undoubtedly changed over the last 20 years. The situation is very similar now to what it was when I started, which is that trustees are unpaid volunteers and they're the ones who are ultimately responsible for the organisation. I think there is a problem with the model now, as it doesn't sufficiently reflect the need to adapt in a rapidly changing environment. We need to move towards a system of integrated governance. You can get towards an integrated governance model with the current arrangements but it's quite cumbersome. You need to make sure that you're delegating sufficiently to the Exec Team, which enables them to make day-to-day decisions without having to refer everything back. It's important to understand that we can't all be trustees; there needs to be something in place make sure that there is non-executive contribution in a way that is helpful and allows for development.

Often trustees are around the age of retirement but the people pushing the boundaries of how organisations work tend to nearer the start of their careers. How do charities access this resource?

Boards need to look for trustees who understand that one of their primary roles is to make sure the organisation is hearing the voices of the beneficiaries, donors, supporters and the public. You don't need to know everything to do that, but you do need to challenge for evidence and ensure all voices are heard. We need to move away from the idea that we must have a representation of everything. Fundamentally, the key thing is not to take that as being a substitute for proper engagement at an operational level.

Every member of the board should understand what people are there to do and stand up for the rights of the beneficiaries to make sure their interests are served as well as they possibly can be. You've got to be prepared to hear other people's voices, look at problems from other people's perspectives and challenge the Exec Team to make sure the words of the beneficiaries don't get filtered out.

What advice would you give to your 20- to 30-year old self?

Expect the unexpected and be able to drop things and move on to something else because the world is like that. Building resilience is also important. Increasingly now, you start off on a career path and in 40 years' time you will end up doing something you never expected. The more open minded you are, the more you can commit yourself to lifelong learning.

What can the armed forces learn from the charity sector?

Although I left 18 years ago, I think there's some obvious feedback around looking at skills and talents rather than looking at what someone's specialism is. The other is about the rank structure, which is important in some situations but there are areas of the military that are more in common with the outside world in terms of bringing talent in. If you haven't been wearing the uniform for 10 to 15 years, then your credentials seem weak.

You've had a successful career, rising to CEO of a couple of organisations. What's given you the foundation and resilience to keep on delivering in those roles?

Apart from having a personal connection to the two charities I've worked for, I think you have to understand how long things take and be there for the long-term. You need to be able to provide stability but there also need to be the agility to respond to circumstances. You also need to give yourself enough time for you because, if you're constantly maxed out, you become jaded. The best thing a previous boss of mine in the navy said to me was, 'remember that this navigation machine you're using needs fuel, rest and oil – it needs looking after.' It took me a while to realise that he was talking about me. I think it's important to make sure that you're building in enough time for you because there will be times when you're so busy that you won't be able to do this. You need to build in time for things that aren't directly connected with work.

Interview: DE, London

As a leader, if you can convey that you really believe in the work you are doing, I think that is motivating for people.

Natalie Acton and Ella Joseph

POSITION AT TIME OF INTERVIEW:
Co-CEOs of Think Ahead. Mental health charity (UK-based)

Natalie Acton and Ella Joseph are Joint CEOs of Think Ahead, a charity which recruits and trains people to become mental health social workers.

Think Ahead places its participants in mental health trusts and local authorities across England, training them to become outstanding mental health social workers who can make a real difference to people with mental health problems.

Natalie and Ella founded Think Ahead together following careers as senior managers in a range of public sector organisations including Government departments (HM Treasury, Department for Education, 10 Downing Street Policy Unit) and local authorities.

It is very rare to have joint CEOs, working on a job-share basis, but we think this approach is likely to be replicated in many other places throughout the 2020s.

Let's take it from the start. How did you both meet?
N: We both worked in the Civil Service for a number of years and met briefly in the Department for Education where we both worked. I left the Civil Service to set up Think Ahead and, within weeks of starting to set it up, I discovered I was pregnant. We were being incubated in a Think Tank and the director suggested that I find a job share partner to make sure that this organisation could work and so that I could come back part-time after I had the baby. Coming back part-time was my choice. I knew that Ella had similar interests to me, but we weren't friends at the time; we'd never actually worked directly with each other.

There were people around you pointing you in the direction of each other.
E: I was on maternity leave and about to go back to the civil service but not feeling wholly excited by the prospect, and Natalie's text arrived.

N: I just texted her and said, 'this is a bit strange but, do you remember me, and would you like to leave your current job and set up a completely new organisation? Don't know if we'll actually be funded but do you want to give it a go?' Ella replied saying, 'yes!'

E: It was just amazing. I felt like I wanted a new challenge and this seemed ideal.

What was it that attracted you to Think Ahead?
E: I felt like it was a luxurious challenge; being tasked with setting something up from scratch but, rather than having to do it from the beginning of a start-up process with lots of funding pitches, we arrived in this amazingly lucky position where we already had seed-funding and the opportunity to be incubated by a successful charity. It just felt like an absolute no brainer for me to jump into.

N: I had been interested in mental health for a while. I had done a post-graduate qualification in Adult Psychotherapy but realised that I really like working in a team, which you don't get to do as an individual psychotherapist. Ella and I really enjoy managing people and really wanted the chance to develop our leadership in a smaller organisation than the civil service.

E: This was an opportunity for us to hone in on supporting the development of a really important bit of the public sector workforce that, in a government department, you're never really close enough to and therefore you can't really effect change in the way that we've been able to.

N: So, there was a bit of luck, and good timing.

Joint CEOs are unusual. How do you make it work?
E: I think the first thing to say is that we're not following a rule book or a pattern or advice that we've been given elsewhere. Because, as you say, it's quite unusual. I think what's quite idiosyncratic about this situation is that – from not knowing each other at all – the absolute fit in terms of our working style, our judgement, the way that we like to work with other people, is such a good match that a lot of the tension, time and effort that people who job share have in handing stuff over and making sure you're on the same page, we just don't have.

How long have you been doing it?
N: Almost five years.

Five years – that's brilliant!
N: I think it works because we're both motivated by very similar things; and because we share a similar professional background, having both been civil servants, we have a very similar way of wanting to manage and run the organisation. Ella is probably one of the people I trust most in the world. I've really learnt that your ego becomes very different when you job share because your performance must be about the outcome, not about your own personal reputation. For example, if either of us does a media interview really well, the other is delighted – there's no place at all for personal ego, we're a total team. It's a different relationship from having a manager or an employee because, in a totally non-hierarchical way, you're so reliant on that person and they're so reliant on you.

How have you built up that trust?
E: It's an interesting question because I don't feel like I came into it unsure of how it would pan out. I jumped in with complete trust right from the beginning.

So, you jumped in with absolute positive intent, both of you?
N: We did.

E: 100%.

E: We have such a similar career background, and our outlook and interests are also extremely similar. We also have the same sense of humour. So, we spend very little time having to explain our position to each other – we usually just 'get it'. I mean obviously we have those sorts of conversations, but we don't have to be constantly thinking about whether we are going to be on the same page. The assumption is always that we will be. If we're not, we'll have a quick conversation just to iron out any differences, but it isn't an uphill struggle.

How do you make it work practically? What's the rhythm of your week?

N: We split the week rather than the job. Ella works Monday to Wednesday, and I work Wednesday to Friday, so we overlap one day a week on a Wednesday. We hand over to each other at the end of our slots but we're in constant contact. Our agreement is that whoever is 'commander-in-the-field' has complete control. Having said that, the commander-in-the-field quite often thinks, 'I wouldn't mind just chewing that over with Ella!'

E: It means that we take the hit of making sure we can give a completely common front to anyone who's dealing with us. So, anyone who talks to one of us can feel like they've spoken to both of us and similarly a decision that one of us takes will not unravel when it's the other one's day. So, anything that we feel the other one might have a view on, we take offline and then we can feed back a robust, consensus view.

E: We've resisted splitting the job because, apart from anything else, we wanted to know that if a trustee phones one of us, or if we have to speak to a minister or someone else at any time, there's not one scintilla of hesitation or doubt in any area of the business. We just don't think it works when you've got a Chief Executive who can't answer, so we've resisted the idea of dividing projects between us, and I feel confident that was the right decision.

Does sharing the job of CEO allow you to balance your lives, your home and your professional lives?

N: We both feel very lucky because it does allow us to work part-time and look after our kids on the other days. I feel especially lucky because my kids are younger and it's hard with small kids to have everything running smoothly all the time. A few months ago, my closest friend was gravely ill in hospital and I had this terrible childcare squeeze and the person who rescued me was Ella. She came to my house and looked after my children. The boundaries are quite loose really and unbelievably supportive.

What would be your advice for others who are looking at job sharing at a senior level?

E: My first piece of advice, based on this experience, is to hold out to find the person you've got that level of fit with; not just in terms of seeing eye to eye and having similarities in outlook, judgment and motivation but also someone you can imagine trusting like that. Part of what makes this all so good is that we love each other's company, we make each other laugh and, if we're having a bad time or a bad meeting, we can see the funny side of it.

E: From my experience of a job share, leadership is more confident and thoughtful because you've got someone to talk to and bounce ideas off.
N: Be clear about the benefits which job-sharing will bring and take time to find the right partnership.

E: And, interestingly, it's as much the men as the women who've met us professionally who say that it's really nice to see a senior job share. It's not just a 'returning to work after maternity leave' conundrum.

Looking back, what advice would you give your 20-year-old self?
N: I think the experience of doing Think Ahead has taught me loads of things. As we're a graduate scheme, one thing I've learnt is the amount of opportunities that are out there for graduates. I'd tell my 20-year-old self to look widely for a variety of opportunities, and not to stick with a particular career path just because you have invested time and energy in it if it no longer brings you joy.

E: I think it's basically not to be scared of change and to always push yourself to do something different.

N: Don't settle if it's not right.

Who has been a mentor for you in your career?
E: You. [Sharon Rice-Oxley, Partner at Q5] I've had managers who have been good or bad and you learn from the bad ones as well as the good ones. But in terms of people who have invested in me and my endeavour at work, tried to help me make a success of it and been interested and thoughtful throughout, absolutely you.

N: My second line manager in the Treasury, who remains a close friend, has always been a mentor to me. One of the things that he has always been incredibly good at is giving pretty much immediate, really good feedback. I can remember having to do an external presentation and I was relatively new to the Treasury and I practised in front of him; I was quite pleased with how it had gone, but he said it was terrible and then told me all the reasons why it was terrible. Although it was a bit of a jolt, there's nothing more helpful than somebody that you trust telling you the truth.

How would you describe your leadership style?
E: From the start we knew the importance of building and maintaining a great team at Think Ahead. What matters to me as a leader of this charity is creating an organisation that lives the values that we believe in. What we've set out to do is create a nurturing and supportive work environment that is very interested in people's personal lives and supports them to fulfil their family commitments.

I hope people who work here feel that we have not just tried to behave like that ourselves, but we have also created a culture where that way of working is the norm. I think it is so important to work in a place that people enjoy and have fun in, but also work hard and get lots out of it personally.

N: As a leader, if you can convey that you really believe in the work you are doing, I think that is motivating for people. Sometimes, in a very large organization, people don't feel control over what they are doing, and cynicism can breed, whereas in an organisation with such a clear mission and which can allow for flexibility and diversity, it can be easier to motivate people.

E: We both take a lot of pride in people having successful careers – people who work for us growing, possibly moving onto other places, but feeling like we've had a positive impact on their long-term career and how they've developed.

What's the naughtiest thing you've ever done?

N: I was once arrested for protesting against veal exports. I was sitting in a road; I was only 16 or 17. Seven of us sat in the back of a police van. Fortunately, they decided not to press charges and we were released. But the naughtiest thing about it was that I'd bunked off school to do it!

E: I can't think of anything naughty that I've done that I'd like to share …

N: Well, she steals my pens …

E: I'm a kleptomaniac for good stationery!

Interview: SR-O, London

As a leader, if you can convey that you really believe in the work you are doing, I think that is motivating for people.

You can have it all, you just can’t have it all at once.

Helen Nash

POSITION AT TIME OF INTERVIEW:
Non-Exec Director of Metcash. Australia's Leading Wholesaler (Australia-based)

Helen Nash is an Independent Non-Executive Director at Metcash, Southern Cross Austereo, Blackmores, Inghams and previously Pacific Brands. She started her career as a Brand Manager at Procter & Gamble (P&G), before moving to IPC Media and subsequently becoming Chief Operating Officer at McDonald's Australia. In this interview, she discusses her formative years at Procter & Gamble, uprooting her life and career to Australia, and her love of *The Shawshank Redemption*.

You have a spent a lot of time working in B2C organisations on brand and marketing. Is that something that you always wanted to do?
Yes, I was drawn to it by an almost innate pull; I suppose you would call it a passion. It was through my exposure to P&G that I got into B2C. I actually joined P&G in the Finance department because I felt rationally that a certified management accountancy qualification, which was on offer through P&G, would be a really safe and sensible thing to do after university.

What did you study at university?
Combined honours in Social Sciences, Psychology, Economics and Management… which translates as I basically played hockey!

What hockey position did you play? …and how did you get into brands?
I played left-midfield. So, I did two years in Finance in order to complete all my exams, but I intuitively felt that I wanted to be part of creating what brands stood for in the consumer's eyes. I wanted to understand through the P&G model the blend of art and science that is involved. It was positioned very much as an art, but with principles and a strategic approach that they could teach you to create advertising that works and is highly compelling to consumers.

What was the best ad campaign that you worked on in your time at P&G?
I was lucky enough to be part of the Pantene brand team as an Assistant Brand Manager, and then my first Brand Manager shift was on Pantene styling. It was an incredible journey of growth. I was involved in one of the country's largest sampling campaigns with a £10 million budget when I was 23; sending sachets through people's doors then ultimately creating the advertising for the Pantene styling launch. I was really proud of that. Then I worked on new brand innovation – New Product Development – and ended up bringing two new hair care brands through the qualification process. The technology was then rolled into Pantene. It was an incredible seven and a half years, and I see that as the foundation of my entire career. I look on it as an incredible gift that I spent that time in that incredible company; I could easily still be there.

Who did you look up to most at P&G?
The largest influence on me was the General Manager of the Health and Beauty Care business at Weybridge when we opened that office, a gentleman called Tim Penner. I remember when he left P&G; that was a real stark realisation that even the great move on. He personified everything that I wanted to be in a leader: he was incredibly smart, but he was even nicer than he was smart, and he was a real gentleman. He built an incredible, positive culture focused on people; and he achieved

phenomenal results in that part of the business. There would be no other way of talking about it other than we would have walked over broken glass for him!

Why did you leave P&G?

The truth of the matter is that I ended up working for a woman who was the complete opposite of everything that makes a good leader I just talked about. She was a bully, and I decided to leave. I was working at that time for P&G in Geneva. In summary: I was 28, single, Geneva was very dull, I had a boss who was a bully, and I was headhunted back to a job at AOL Time Warner in the UK; so really there were a combination of push and pull factors.

Isn't it interesting that so many people join a brand, but they leave due to a manager?

It came down to culture again because I found out subsequently that she was asked to leave, and I was the seventh person that she had lost. P&G, of course, acted on that. It takes a long time to build a culture, and it takes just weeks and months to destroy it; it's so fragile. I wouldn't change that experience because the learning that it gave me was that I won't tolerate bullies. Culture trumps strategy.

How long were you in the UK for?

Three years, and I went through my first ever acquisition. The business I joined was IPC Media, which was a print business, and I came back as marketing director of the women's monthly magazines. The interesting thing about that business is that it had stated a desire to move from a publishing-led business to a marketing-led business. The marketing directors of other divisions and I were brought in at the same time to be part of this shift from publishing-led to marketing-led. That was an incredibly exciting, challenging journey to go on. At the end of those three years, the business was very successfully sold to AOL Time Warner.

Knowing when to leave is important, isn't it? It sounds like you're very conscious of that.

My head-hunter and boss at the time said, 'this is the journey that we want to go on'. I looked back on that at the end of the three years culminating in the sale of the business and decided we had done what we set out to achieve. There was also a change in leadership at group level and I could see a reversion back to being a publishing culture and a publishing-led business. I decided it was not a journey that I needed or wanted to be a part of.

So, you took the big bold decision to resign and head to Australia... via a circuitous Asian diving route. You then built your career in Australia very successfully and now you're into your third chapter.

I had the executive chapter here, which again was really the catalyst of the single most important person in my Australian career, Peter Bush. He had come in as the coach to Guy Russo, CEO of McDonalds at the time. Guy had the huge self-awareness to say that he didn't know how to turn the business around. McDonalds had been in a 10-year decline, and Peter Ritchie, the Chairman, gave Guy names of three potential coaches; Peter Bush was the person that Guy chose. Then, Guy convinced Peter to become COO of the business and Peter ultimately took over from Guy when he went to China. I came in when Peter was transitioning from COO to CEO. I met Peter - I wasn't supposed to meet him, I was meant to meet one of his direct reports, but the diaries got messed up. There are so many things in life that are about who you meet and when you meet them. I think he looked primarily at my Procter training and thought maybe she'll be a bit useful; and we got on very well. He should be credited with really establishing talent development and succession planning within McDonalds, and shining a light on the high potential talent many, many layers down in the organisation and cross-functionally.

... finding high potential individuals is a real art, and so few organisations get that right.

So few get it right – and so few prioritise it, because everyone tends to want to focus on the here and now and not think about the future. He really knew that there was an incredible bed of talent waiting to be discovered – the business employed 90,000 people.

What gets you out of bed in the morning?

So many things: my daughter, my horse, my dog... ultimately, a sense of enormous guilt that my husband gets up at 5:30am to ride his bike. I applaud him for it but I'm not a morning person, so I get out of bed at about 6:55am because I think that's respectable and not too lazy. In terms of a more philosophical answer to that question, what gets me up is that I've now got an extraordinary balance in my life. I feel incredibly grateful for how I get to spend my time and the majority of the time, I have a really fabulous day to look forward to.

So, there's a genuine motivation. You don't end up doing stuff that you don't want to do?

We all have tasks in our life that we don't like doing. There will always be a proportion of that – mine is quite low.

You've worked hard to get that, no doubt.
I have, and I'm very protective of it. I very often get asked what CEO job I would give it up for, and there isn't one. There aren't enough hours in the day to do a job like that and do the other things that I value so much.

What advice would you give to your 20-year-old self?
I think it comes back to what we were talking about – chapters. I think that you can absolutely have it all over a period of different chapters in your life, depending on how you define 'all at the same time'. I would say, if you're interested in having a career, go and burn it. You're young and you've got energy and you're probably not married, and you've probably not got kids, so don't worry about all of that. If it feels right to be working hard at that time, then do it and for goodness sake don't work for bullies! Go and work with purpose and passion. Work really hard and become really, really good at what you do. When I was 20, there certainly was a very clear understanding that anything worth having in life took time to earn. Generations now have a very different expectation in that they think they can have it all and have it now. I would say to myself if I was a millennial now that the important things in life – the things that are worth having – take time and graft and persistence and passion, and that doesn't happen overnight.

You've alluded to having mentors and people who've had an impact on you. Can you pinpoint one person that has had a major impact on you?
It would absolutely have to be Peter Bush. He believed in me more than I believed in myself. It's an amazing gift to give someone and now I have to try to somehow be that for somebody else.

Being a very successful woman – has that ever been in the way?
Because I was in that positive environment for so long at McDonalds and most of the time at P&G, I never felt the gender issue. I think if I roll it back up, it would be to make sure that you really understand the culture of an organisation as you look to join it, and make sure that it fits with the values that you hold as an individual. If you get the people and the culture right, you can create the vision and the mission and the strategy.

What is your favourite film?
That's so easy - *The Shawshank Redemption*.

That's an amazing film. How many times have you seen it?
Probably four; not that many. It's such a boring answer because I'm sure it comes up time and time again. For me though, I'm a glass half-full person and I need to have a happy ending.

I've taken us off the business track. This idea of chapters – can you just say a word on that?
If you think of things on the platform along the timeline of forever, that can be very frightening. If you can break things down, whether it is a work chapter or a geographical chapter, then it becomes so much more manageable, and you can attach objectives and goals around different chapters of your life. I think, for me, it gives great validity to the idea that you can have it all, you just can't have it all at once. I'm sure that it applies to men as well, but I think that there is a huge amount of pressure right now on women to do it all, juggle it all, and I do think that it is unfair. I think if you are trying to hold down a career and be a great wife and a great parent and have something separate that's your own personal passion at the same time, that's really, really hard. I decided that I couldn't do that and didn't want to do that. But I think if you look at a chapter and ask yourself what's important for me, or if you're in a family unit, what's important for us in this next chapter, you can break it down. It becomes so much more manageable and you can see what success looks like, which is no different to how you'd approach a business.

Yes, but applying it into your own life?
We often apply our brains, rationale and strategy so well to a business and yet, we don't do it to our own personal lives. The same tools apply and can have just as big of an impact, if not more, given that it affects you personally.

Interview: TL, Sydney

Go and work with purpose and passion. Work really hard and become really, really good at what you do.

It's not education … work … retirement. Your life is much more flexible than that. Education is something that occurs all the way through your life, in different ways.

Jonathan Powell

POSITION AT TIME OF INTERVIEW:
Founder and CEO of Inter Mediate. A leader in mediation and negotiation (UK-based)

Jonathan Powell has had a storied career in negotiation, from working on the Hong Kong Handover and German Unification in the Foreign Office, to serving as chief negotiator in Northern Ireland whilst he was Tony Blair's Chief of Staff.

He now heads Inter Mediate, an NGO that specialises in bringing together governments and insurgents to negotiate an end to armed conflicts. In this interview he discusses his experiences in the high-stakes world of politics, negotiation, and even a brief stint in investment banking which he admitted to being "too sedate" for him.

What first excited you about politics in the beginning of your career?

I had always been very political. Even as a schoolboy I was fascinated by politics. My real baptism was when I went to Washington, aged 17, to work as the second undergardener at the British Embassy. My brother was private secretary to the ambassador so I went every morning to mow the lawn. It was 1973, year of the Watergate Tapes. My brother was good friends with the journalists who were covering the White House at the time and they came back every evening with the Watergate transcripts and plonked them on the kitchen table for me to read. My induction to politics was "don't do cover-up because a cover-up always gets you in the end". When I was covering politics for the British Embassy in America from '91 to '94, I attached myself to Bill Clinton. I chose Bill because he had been at my college at Oxford. I initially travelled around with him in a minibus, where he was an execrable public speaker who eventually became one of the best in the world. That is what really got me into politics.

The world of politics though wasn't your first job, was it? I understand that you were initially a journalist.

I started as a journalist at Granada TV but got fed up because I was having a terrible time there. Although through Tony Wilson I got to meet the Sex Pistols, New Order, and others that he brought into the studio. I then applied to the Foreign Office because my parents thought journalism wasn't a proper job. The Foreign Office accepted me, and I agonised for a bit, before deciding to go off and join them.

No one joins the foreign office unless they are interested in travel, is that true for you?

My father was in the Air force, so I grew up in Singapore and Malaysia. Travel was nothing new, and I loved it. From a very early age I started travelling by myself. At 14 I was travelling around Italy, completely on my own. But that wasn't the reason why I applied. My older brother was in the Foreign Office and my parents were worried about things like pensions. They felt I should work in an "establishment" kind of career.

I was in the embassy in Washington and I'd been a political officer following Clinton. I had been looking to see if I could get a Labour seat as an MP, but it was very difficult from abroad. Blair wanted to meet Clinton and I was able to introduce the two of them. Blair, when he unexpectedly became leader of the Labour Party, asked me if I would consider being his Chief of Staff. I quit the foreign office and went to work in the Labour Party. At the time it was in a complete 'start-up' state. John Smith had died. There was no money, no office, no staff. We had to build the whole thing up.

My youth was defined by eighteen years of continuous Conservative rule. The 1997 UK General Election was quite a plate-tectonic shift. How did it feel on the inside of the Labour machine?

Funnily enough, I was asked in an interview recently, "With Boris Johnson winning a great majority, is it the same feeling as Blair coming in in '97?" I replied, "Well, I don't think so! It doesn't feel like there's the outpouring of joy on the streets, that we felt back in '97". They then said, "It's just London." But I don't think that's true. You look around and don't see people out on the streets celebrating.

What was the highlight of your time working at Downing Street?

The most important thing for me was the Northern Ireland Peace Agreement, both signing the Good Friday Agreement in 1998, and more importantly, getting it implemented in May '2007. That was a lifetime's labour. It was an incredible feeling when we got McGuinness and Paisley together for the first time. That was the highest point for me.

Would you say the Northern Ireland Peace Agreement was the greatest success of the Blair government?

It's certainly the greatest unsung success of the Blair government. Even now with Brexit, no one really understands Ireland. No one pays any attention to Northern Ireland which is why it's such a tragedy that people now are trying to screw it up.

Do you think the majority government Boris secured (12th Dec 2019) threatens the Good Friday Agreement?

There is certainly a threat. The good news is that it is <u>not</u> the catastrophic threat that Boris made with his own proposal for the Brexit deal. He tried to propose that there should be a border between Northern Ireland and the rest of Ireland; that really would have been catastrophic. It might well have led right back into conflict. The problem is that we have now created an economic border between Northern Ireland and the rest of the United Kingdom, and that threatens the identity of Unionists, who want to remain in the United Kingdom. There is likely to be a big political crisis again because they have reopened the issue of identity.

What was the most challenging aspect of being the chief negotiator for the Northern Ireland peace process?

It was a very difficult experience. There I was, trying to be Chief of Staff to Tony Blair, running Number 10, and crossing the Irish Sea once a week. I would go and meet Adams and McGuinness in safe houses, and then go and meet the Unionist Leaders. Often the negotiations would go on through the night. They were very tough. The hardest thing of all was to build trust. There I was, an English public-school boy, a conventional establishment figure, trying to win the trust of two Republican Terrorists and Unionists who had even greater suspicions about the British. The real challenge was how to persuade people like this that you're being straight with them. I remember Gerry Adams leaning across the table on a really tough day and he said, "Jonathan, the thing I like about you is that when you lie, you blush." My Northern Irish Office colleague sitting next to me struck back with "Unlike you, Gerry!" Building that trust with both sides was the key challenge. It's why I've gone into this business subsequently. It's not something everyone can do. But if you've got the ability, then it's worth making something of.

But you didn't set up your Intermediate after Tony Blair stepped down, you moved to Morgan Stanley?
I knew that once Tony was out, I couldn't go back to being a civil servant. The only people who were offering me jobs back then were banks. I was initially going to go to JP Morgan but then Tony Blair went there at the last minute, so I switched to Morgan Stanley. I lasted a year there, but didn't do very much really. I wrote two books and did a few TV programs. I didn't do much banking. I quit after that, because I really wasn't enjoying it. I didn't really have what it took to be a banker.

Did you miss the excitement of Government? After having been working at Number 10 on all sorts of sensitive and confidential things, was the world of banking quite sedate compared to your average week in Downing Street?
What I couldn't get used to in the private sector, was how little work people do or appear to do. All my career, I have been working a 16-hour day every day and weekends, even more so in Downing Street. So, I couldn't get used to the sedate pace of life. There are some amazing people doing banking. But, I think some of the talents are wasted in that sector, particularly the younger ones. When you go into these huge rooms of people speaking Russian, Turkish, Chinese, all fluently, I am gobsmacked by how good they are.

What were the drivers that made you set up Inter Mediate?
Even before I left number 10, I had been working on the ETA conflict in Spain. I had been approached by a guy called Martin Griffiths, who was head of the Centre for Humanitarian Dialogue. They had been working between ETA and the Spanish Government trying to get a deal. However, it was about to collapse. So they came to Downing Street to see if I could help. The year I was at Morgan Stanley I was also going back and forth to the Basque region, and it gave me a real taste for it again. A bit like Eeyore, I discovered what I really like; and what I really like is thistles.

Winning consulting business needs a lot of shoe leather and 'getting out there'. In your work, how do these opportunities, such as dealing with ETA or going to Afghanistan, come about?
Normally we insert ourselves into a conflict. Sometimes people come to us, increasingly because they might now know what we're doing. But usually it's happenstance.

Are there competitors to Inter Mediate?
Yes, but they aren't really in the same field. I determined very early on that we weren't going to be a large organisation. Having run a large organisation in the British government, the last thing I wanted to do was to be responsible for management. So, I capped the number of people we would have, keeping it small and personal. There are competitors, but they're much bigger and do different things. The one we broke away from, the Centre for Humanitarian Dialogue, has grown very big now. It gets involved with lots of conflicts and has lots of staff and regional offices all over the place. We focus on only one very narrow thing, which is taking leaders of governments and armed groups and trying to get them to talk to each other.

Who have been the biggest influences on your career to date?
Bill Clinton and Tony Blair have been very important. Bill got me into politics. Having followed him around I wanted to be a practitioner. Tony gave me the chance to work at the centre of things. If I think back to people who influenced me at the Foreign Office, there was Percy Cradock, ambassador to China and the negotiator on Hong Kong, I was a desk officer at the time. Percy had extraordinary intellect and an incredible ability to negotiate. He certainly had a big impact on my interest in that field. I would never have expected to spend my life doing negotiations. It was doing the Hong Kong Handover with him that propelled me in that direction.

What advice would you give to those at the very beginning of their adult lives as they start exploring the world of work?
I would give two pieces of advice. One is don't think in terms of a straight-line progression; you're unlikely to start on something and do it for the rest of your life. When I started in the 1970s, it was never going to be a straight progression. I think I would have been quite bored if it had been. It's not education .... work .... retirement. Your life is much more flexible than that. Education is something that occurs all the way through your life, in different ways. Think about it as a series of modules in which you are going to do different things at various stages. Make sure you acquire the skills to do the things you want to do.

My second bit of advice is to do the things that you find interesting. Money is not the be-all and end-all. I know that many don't have the option of doing what they love. That said, if you do have that opportunity, make the most of it, and choose the interesting thing over the well-paid thing.

Interview: OP

People say that in order to make it you have to have lost it; I disagree with that. I think that you can learn from other people's mistakes.

Olly Olsen

POSITION AT TIME OF INTERVIEW:
Founder and co-CEO of The Office Group. Office Space (UK-based)

Olly Olsen is Co-CEO of The Office Group, a business at the forefront of the flexible office revolution in the UK when they started in 2003. Q5 itself joined the ranks in February, opening a state-of-the-art TOG office in Leeds. Olly and his business partner Charlie Green sold a majority stake in the company to Blackstone in a reported £500 million deal in 2018. In this interview, Olly talks about his life as an entrepreneur and CEO.

Did you always have the 'fire of the entrepreneur' within you, or did it hit you later in life?
I'd like to think it's always been there, and I suppose it's come from two things: myself, but also my family and upbringing. I remember at a very young age hearing about my late grandfather and how wonderful he was. He was a very successful property developer in the 60s who passed away at a young age at the high point of his career. He became well known and people still talk about him today. Hearing about his success and reputation was really important for me. It gave me the motivation to work hard and have confidence in my ability from an early age. At 12, I was working paper rounds and, at 14, I had several different jobs. I left school at a very young age and didn't pass any of my GCSEs. At 16, I was working full-time with three or four jobs on the go: pizza delivery, night security watchman, market trading - as soon as I had a licence, I was selling stuff out of the back of my car.

Sounds like your grandfather was a big influence on you, who else influenced you and what did you learn from them?
People say that in order to make it you have to have lost it; I disagree with that. I think that you can learn from other people's mistakes. I looked up to my parents in very different ways. My mother was always honest with us, which made me realise the benefit of being open with everyone I meet. My father instilled the simple importance of hard graft, and I've inherited that from him. My uncle – who gave me my first job in this sector – also played a big part in steering me. This says to me that you must take help wherever you can get it. Don't try and do it all on your own – only do it on your own when you really need to. My family were probably the biggest early influences; more recently, our ex-Chairman Lloyd Dorfman, has been a big help and support.

So, after leaving school, did you go straight into business?
I spent 9 months working out in LA, and at 21 I decided to spend 2 years travelling the world on my own, after saving up the money to go. I'd been paying my family rent for 2 years and the week before I left, my parents gave me a cheque back for that amount. That moment signified a lot. For my parents it was about the principle: you've got to pay your way, but they wanted me to travel and experience the world.

And that's where you met your business partner Charlie?
Yes, in Thailand! I was on the beach and said 'hello', then a few years later, Charlie and I were working together at MWB.

There is a stereotype of young people travelling the world and 'drifting' – were you tempted to stay out there?
I wanted life experiences. All my friends were at university, which didn't seem like much fun. When I left and got on the plane I knew exactly where I was going, exactly what I wanted to do, exactly what I wanted to

experience, exactly when I was coming home and what I was going to do when I came back. It was all part of my plan. I've always given myself roughly two, three, four and five-year plans. I gave myself a plan to go away, to have a fabulous time, to come back, to work hard and to start a business. There was no risk of me drifting, it's not really in my nature.

What did you do when you got back?
I waited tables and then I slowly got into other sectors. I was a debt collector; I went into the fashion business as a salesman. Then my uncle bought into a serviced office business and asked me to come and interview for it. I went in and interviewed to start work on the phones – I was 26 at that time. I got myself a job right at the very bottom and decided that, in 4 to 5 years' time, I wanted to be a big earner, a more senior person in this team, or to have learnt enough to be able to do it myself.

What was the spark for the idea of The Office Group?
I was fortunate enough to be on the shop floor, showing people workspace. And because I was selling the workspace, I was able to understand first-hand what the consumer was asking for. When Starbucks arrived on the high street, office users started to leave their buildings to hold informal meetings there. The phrase 'let's go for coffee', as opposed to 'let's go for a meeting', started. Office buildings were no longer just desks, meeting rooms, and reception areas; there were lounges, comfortable furniture, bean bags and sofas. It was clear the design of office space needed to change. There really was no option for a small to medium sized business to take workspace on flexible terms, other than serviced offices which were deemed to be impersonal, expensive and offering no value whatsoever. I felt that I could do it far better.

Co-CEOs are relatively unusual – how has that relationship evolved?
It was really clear to me when Charlie and I started how we would both add value, and there was no cross-over between what we did. We said if we're going to do this, the one relationship that will make or break it is ours and our trust in each other. If we agree from the outset that we will have a relationship for life where we can tell each other anything, we will have a far greater chance of success.

Has that trust been strained at any point?
Charlie and I are very different people and work in very different ways. We sometimes disagree, but we always listen to each other and we respect each other's views. We will never disagree in front of others. I think we've been fortunate enough to make the right decisions. The strain has come in the past around big decisions, investor changes and the direction of the business. Charlie has a brilliant reputation in the industry – arguably the best reputation of anyone I know – and I have a pretty good instinctive nature about what move to make. We trust each other and it works very well.

Have you been able to take time to recognise the journey so far?

One thing Charlie and I had never done was really celebrated our success together. When you've been through a journey like we have, the highs and lows, you need to share it. You can share it with family and friends, but it's not the same as sharing it with someone you've done it with and experienced it with. Recently Charlie and I went away together to celebrate what we've achieved – and it was really one of the most special times, being able to pat each other on the back.

What is the biggest challenge for growing the business?

This business won't grow without us delegating to the next level of senior management. I've always recognised that you need to surround yourself with people that can add value. I'd like to think that the emotion and outlook that Charlie and I have is infectious to everyone else. If we're tired, fed up, nervous, it's like wildfire. It's infectious. When Charlie and I are buzzing with excitement, everyone else is exactly the same. So, if you›re having a bad day, hide it … or don't come in!

What are the characteristics and attributes that you look for in the people you work with?

I look for people who are calm, honest, loyal, hard-working and trustworthy. And that's over and above any qualifications or experience. When we interview, I sit down with someone and if I connect with them on a social basis and enjoy being around the person, it's a win. Or rather, if I'm not connecting with that person on an emotional basis, or a social basis, then we won't even go through to the second stage, irrespective of how much experience they have. It's a marriage, we want them to want us as much as we want them.

How do you motivate and engage the next generation of people entering the workforce?

Recently, a number of people have chosen to stay with the business but have a change of scenery, taking a salary cut in order to do this. The fact is that it is not just about money for the next generation. We are able to give individuals a reason to get up in the morning and a purpose – everyone is very aware of what we are here to provide, who we're up against and what our purpose is every day – which seems to be about giving our employees a reason to be here, which is not about the money.

What advice would you have for someone starting out in the industry fresh from school?

You have to differentiate yourself from the chasing pack; there are a lot of people doing what we're doing now. When we started this business, there weren't many people offering flexible workspace. I would say, make sure you differentiate yourself and, if you can do that, you should be able to pick up part of the market-share.

Is there anything that you look back on and think, 'if I had my time again, I'd do that differently'?
I never, ever look back and think we could have done it differently. I could have negotiated a better deal on the very first deal – slightly more equity – but not for one minute do I regret anything that I've done. I'd have to think really hard about what I'd change. I think I'm very privileged and very lucky to have that mindset. Of course, we've made mistakes. I reckon there are a few points here and a few tweaks there that I could have made, but that's not what it's about.

How do you get the balance right between everything you need to do as a leader of a business and getting the time you need for other things, like getting your mojo back and spending time with family?
We care about balance, and we've always given all our employees the ability to do whatever needs to be done and take time off when needed. Days off, whether it's birthdays – and everyone does get time off for their birthday – or time off for other things, we recognise the need for mental wellbeing. Health is everything, and I don't think mental health is given enough focus. I'm physically fit, but if I'm stressed then I'm not able to operate properly. We recognise it, and I think our teams would feel that we give them enough room to find their own work-life balance.

There's an interesting role modelling piece – getting the balance right between showing that you're both in it and as passionate as ever, but also that you will take time for other things.
I recently spent a week's holiday at home, which helped me realise how important that balance is. Every day I wake up super early, and the earlier I'm awake the more excited I am, because I feel I can get onto my emails sooner. It's not healthy. If I'm first in the office, it makes me feel good about myself… which does not help. I don't need to be in at 7.15 in the morning and be the last one to leave. Spending that week at home helped me realise I can get a lot more done if I balance my time.

We use social media; we post pictures and our team sees what we do. They can see that we›re there with our families and we›re enjoying ourselves but that we›re also there for our business. They're equal priorities.

Interview: AC, London

If there's an opportunity to find an intersection between your interests, hobbies, passion and something where you can make some money, that's always a good thing.

Alison Loehnis

POSITION AT TIME OF INTERVIEW:
President of NET-A-PORTER and MR PORTER.
Digital fashion retailer (UK-based)

Alison Loehnis is one of the most influential business leaders in Fashion. She grew up in Manhattan and studied Art History at Brown University. Whilst fashion was always her passion, Alison began her career in advertising at Saatchi & Saatchi in New York in 1992, before embarking on a variety of roles

Witty, stylish, yet reassuringly grounded, Alison has been at the epicentre of digital luxury fashion since the mid '90s. Alison discusses her love of art, and her creative instincts, both of which have been important ingredients in her role as President of Net-A-Porter and Mr Porter.

From the start, what was the thing that initially excited you about fashion?
I've always, always loved clothes. My mother had great taste, took pride in her appearance and got a lot of joy out of what she wore. I think I experienced that through osmosis. I was recently thinking back to my early memories of clothes and fashion. I went to a girls' school with a strict uniform. Before any sort of 'mufti day', I'd be thinking for weeks about what I was going to wear. It wasn't with trepidation, but with excitement. What I realised is that for me, fashion has always been associated with self-expression, fun and choice. I went to a girl's school (with a uniform) for 12 years, and went to a summer camp that also had a uniform. So fashion was an exciting break. I love it and have done so-since I was little.

Yet, despite your love of fashion, it was advertising that first employed you. How did you end up in the world of advertising?
I naively never really thought fashion was something that I could do "for a job". I love art and always wanted to study art history, having been introduced to it my last year of high school. In fact, I thought I'd work in the art business. But when I graduated, the market was totally dead. I'm a very visual person and I love the creative process. However, I've also always been very interested in business. I suppose I was on a search for the perfect balance between business and creativity. Advertising to me seemed like a great first step, because you're looking for visual and creative ways to sell a product, or to solve a problem.

You didn't stay in advertising for long though. Did you gain all you could from it? Or get bored?
I spent a year in advertising at Saatchi & Saatchi, which was such a privilege. Saatchi was a big agency, and very much my professional education. I was given an assistant. I had my own office. I worked with really clever people. I was completely spoiled! But the creative process and income management side were siloed. I found myself pining to be in the room with the people with the 'magic markers'.

My next job was in communications with Hachette Filipacci Magazines (HFM). They were ahead of their time in terms of having just launched a Contract Publishing division. I managed to get my fingers in lots of different pies. I loved the pitching process and I liked working on so many different titles. The training I'd had at Saatchi really helped in terms of presenting and packaging up ideas for audiences that were not always ready to receive them.

So how did you come to work for Disney?
While I was at HFM, I was doing a bit of freelance work on the side for an independent production company in New York. I had a growing interest in film. I was writing 'coverage' for screenplays and scripts. Little

did I know that you can get paid for this; I did it for free and thought they were doing me a really big favour. Anyway, several years into my time at HFM a woman who had joined as the Editor-in-Chief of Premiere magazine was hired by Disney to head up the Motion Picture Office in New York. She asked me if I'd like to come with her.

Given Disney's strong brand heritage, would you say it is more creative or corporate?
I'd say it was a combination. We were a Development Office, and we were tasked with finding intellectual property coming out of New York that could be developed into feature films and, later, television. That could be theatre, journalism, books and so on. So, say you'd written a book, or a novel, and wanted to auction it, our job was to package things up and say, "We've found this great new writer. This is the vision. This is the audience. We think *this* director would be great". We would pitch it to the studio.

When we went in and spoke with producers or the smaller production companies, that process was hugely creative. I think once you then get plugged into the broader Disney operation it may be different, but my experience was that it was well-balanced.

So now to the world of fashion, which you're much more well-known for. How did your move to NET-A-PORTER come about?
I was on maternity leave from LVMH when a head-hunter that I'd known for quite some time called me to catch up. She asked what I was doing. I told her I'd just had a baby and she asked me to visit her for a career catch up. At the end of a very long conversation, she asked whether I'd be interested if anything ever came up at NET-A-PORTER? I bit her hand off! I'd been a customer from the word go, so it was such an exciting proposition for me. I always loved selling; my dream had been to sell a product I was truly passionate about.

Are there any showpiece projects from your 13 years at NET-A-PORTER and MR PORTER that really stand out?
I don't sit still very easily. The fact that I'm in year 13 at The YOOX NET-A-PORTER GROUP shows what an innovative and exciting business this is, with a great new project around every corner. There have also been a number of opportunities created by some of the corporate and ownership structure changes.

Project wise, I'd say one of my high points was the launch of MR PORTER. That was incredibly exciting for a few reasons. We identified a gap in the market, which isn't to say that there wasn't terrific menswear out there. There just wasn't something for the "man in the NET-A-PORTER woman's life". We also work in a very fast-paced and competitive industry and we wanted to get there first. So, we developed it covertly, and moved super-fast. There weren't many of us and we were nimble. I would never say the work is done, I just feel the team did such a superb job on the branding and the execution and built a business that isn't just successful commercially, but also has a huge amount of brand equity. It was a very collegial, fun, intense project and a great product.

Given the traction that The YOOX NET-A-PORTER GROUP now has, do you ever look over to the physical retailers, or mull on the current high street environment and feel thankful that isn't you?
I think no matter where you are, you have your own challenges. Am I happy not to have leases all over the place and physical buildings? Correct. That said, I have different kinds of challenges. I have technology, which is a blessing but also requires significant investment to remain ahead of the game.

One thing that has really snowballed, both online and on the high-street, is how much choice the customer has and the changing expectations around the shopping experience. One of the things I've said to my teams for years is when you look at what your customers expect, don't just look at the world of luxury fashion because that's not the only place people are buying things. While the Amazon experience may not be 'on brand' for everyone, people can now get (and expect) things super-fast. Some of the best customer service I've had comes from players way outside our fashion universe. It's important to be mindful of that now, but it's also important to consider what the customer expectation is, given what they're buying from you.

What advice would you give to your younger self, or someone at the start of their career?
Don't be afraid of making a move, but also be conscious of what your story says. Keep an eye on your CV but don't be slavish to it. The brands and the companies that you work for <u>do matter</u> and you should look to work for companies that are known, have prestige and give you opportunities to grow. I would also say go with your gut. While it doesn't always happen, if there's an opportunity to find an intersection between your interests, hobbies, passion and something where you can make some money, that's always a good thing.

Looking back, are there certain people who have been particularly influential to you?
I would say my parents, particularly my mom who was always incredibly helpful. She was a great sounding board and totally au fait with the working world. My dad has always been my go-to for a confidence boost and help with negotiation. When I went to LVMH I was hired by a man called Francois Steiner. He was brought in by LVMH to run Thomas Pink which was a new acquisition for them. Francois hired me,

at first, as Sales Director and then Sales and Marketing Director. He took a complete punt on me and for that, I will be forever appreciative. We had a great relationship and he remains a dear friend. Francois was tough as hell, but fair and I just wanted to raise my game all the time. He taught me a lot.

There have obviously been others. Mentorship is important and I love providing mentorship. You know, I think it's funny, it's become one of those things where people think, 'oh, gosh, I don't have a mentor, who is my mentor?' I don't think it should a given, but rather if you find someone who is a mentor to you, that's really lucky.

The number of female to male senior leaders is still highly disproportionate. Have you encountered any challenges as a woman in the business world?
Happily, I haven't encountered issues. One of things I'm very proud of, on behalf of The YOOX NET-A-PORTER GROUP, is that over half of the senior management roles are held by women. Our industry tends to attract quite a lot of women and that's something I'm mindful of. I certainly don't take it for granted, because there are some industries and markets which tend to be much more male dominated. I appreciate and am mindful of potential challenges, but I happily haven't found it to be much of a fight personally.

Is the fashion industry as glamorous as it can seem from the outside?
Yes and no. I think the 'yes' is obvious in that we are working with beautiful things. I'd like to think that when you buy something beautiful, it gives you a boost and you feel empowered. That's a great thing. We get to go and see terrific creations from super-talented people from all over the world. So, yes! That said, it is a tough industry. And by that, I mean things move really, really quickly. You have to work really hard. If I think about buying, for example, there used to be only two seasons. Now I've got buyers buying for four seasons, seemingly year-round. You are expected to have your eye on everything and you're constantly on the road.

And finally, as the environmental agenda becomes more prevalent, is one of your main challenges going to be balancing the demands of your customers with the needs of society as a whole?
We have been supporting sustainable brands for a long time at The YOOX NET-A-PORTER GROUP. What I wanted to do is create a place where customers can easily find sustainable brands because, right now, they're sometimes tucked away and not always easy to find. That's why we created a category called 'Net Sustain' which has been terrific. It's a hub for brands who meet a set of standards,

predetermined by NET-A-PORTER; we vet our brands against a framework of sustainable pillars so, for example, their use of considered materials, how they source fabrics, or their waste reduction. It helps our customers understand the provenance of what they're buying and how it was made, both across beauty and fashion. We started with NET-A-PORTER and we have other plans coming soon…

Coming back to overproduction and waste, I think it's possible for a love of clothes and the issue of waste to be separable from one another. I advocate buying well, looking after your clothes, repeat wearing and incorporating the old with the new. The whole circularity movement gives used or unwanted products the second life they deserve.

Interview: OP, London

Don't be afraid of making a move, but also be conscious of what your story says. Keep an eye on your CV but don't be slavish to it.

For me personally – and my friends that I've spoken to about this – there must be something more than waking up and going to work to make money.

Olayinka Aresa

POSITION AT TIME OF INTERVIEW:
Alumnus of Harris Academy and member of Q5 Youth Panel (UK-based)

Yinka Aresa is a member of the Q5 Youth Panel. The Youth Panel was launched in 2018, to draw in promising pupils who had entered their final two years of secondary school. The purpose of the Panel is to get insight from the 'next working generation', to understand what they value in life, and know what matters to them as they prepare to enter the world of work. It's a 'paid gig', with the Panel sitting during school vacations. Yinka was a member of our Youth Panel during the 2018/19 school year.

Yinka is Generation Z. Born in Lagos, Nigeria, Yinka moved to Peckham with his parents when he was ten. In this interview, Yinka discusses what he wants out of his career, gentrification in Peckham and his love of art and design.

Congratulations Yinka, you have just finished school! What lies in store for you next?

I am taking a gap year. The intention is to do everything 'creative' that I've always wanted to do, but exams and school education got in the way! The year out is to focus on my photography, on my writing and all the other creative things that I love to do. I have applied to study Arts, English and History at the University of Warwick. I love these subjects because it allows you to study human nature through very different lenses.

Do you intend to travel at all during your Gap Year?

I've already spent a month doing a 'half-placement' with the British Council. I went to work as an invigilator and to carry out some research for the British Council at the British Pavilion in Venice. That was fun! It was also very interesting. My research focused on how to curate exhibitions for young people in a way that is not patronising, that draws them in and is what they want to see … and not simply what a bunch of people in a room decide what young people want to see.

Talking of your passion for History and Art, is there anyone from history that you view as a great leader?

I have got into Peggy Guggenheim over the last couple of years. She helped to shape what we understand as contemporary and modern art. During the Second World War when artists were fleeing for their lives, especially Jewish artists, a lot of their work was left behind. Peggy Guggenheim collected and protected it, making sure that future generations could experience the creativity and energy that all these artists had given. She collected works from Picasso, Kandinsky, her husband Max Ernst, and others. She helped shape modern art. I'm inspired by her because she is someone who had no idea what she wanted to do early on in her life, but she knew she had a passion for art. Even though she couldn't draw, she knew that what she *could* do was help people who were very creative. She believed in them – that was her purpose in life.

What have you learnt from your brief experience of business after university?

For a long time, I thought there was a certain pathway to get to where I want to be. Although I could still go through the educational route, there are always different ways of getting into it. During my spell on the Youth Panel, speaking to the people we were introduced to during the programme, it was very interesting to find out the different routes they had taken to get to where they were. Also, to use a cliché, you have to believe in yourself. You need to believe in what you are doing, to take a chance and to push stuff. Believing in an idea and going for it is probably the main thing I've learnt so far. I've taken that for granted too often but now I am properly starting to go for it.

On those points, owning your career and having belief in yourself, what do business leaders need to do to attract the top talent of your generation? For instance, is it important for companies to meet you face-to-face at Careers Fairs?
I think those visits are very worthwhile. I'm really interested in law, so I go to law conferences and speak to the recruiters that attend those events. This has really helped me decide which law firm I'd like to apply to in the future; not just the recruiters, but also the kinds of people who are already applying. So far in my Gap Year, I've applied for a lot of jobs but too many of them provide little to no information. It's not clear enough what exactly your role is. In fact, too many of the job descriptions are unclear. It's really important to have conversations with recruiters so that you can ask the questions directly to them early, even before you apply. Building that connection between yourself and the company, that's something that my friends and I talk about, in terms of knowing what your responsibility will be on a day-to-day basis. Job security is also key.

Fast forward... you've secured the job of your dreams. In the Youth Panel sessions, a few of you stressed how important it would be for your generation to "own your own development". Tell us more.
Yes, that's definitely the case. At the moment, I'm working as a Teaching Assistant at my old school. One of the things I talk about with my line manager is what I want to achieve at the end. One of my goals is to get more students reading books, fiction or non-fiction, it doesn't matter. I also want to get more students interested in humanities subjects. Currently, they do it because it is expected of them, even if they have no interest in them. Just those few examples I have given about what I want to achieve, motivates me to work more. I go into lessons and help out the teachers and mentor the students. I know that's my job description but having those two additional goals that I've given myself, makes me work even harder because I have some autonomy.

What do you want to see from your leaders both now and in the future?
I would say openness. I understand that levels of authority need to be clear, but they also need to be human. To use galleries as an example, it seems to me that too many people who work in them seem to be miserable! I love art, so I visit galleries in London regularly. The people who work there are getting paid something like £16 an hour, but too many of them don't appear to care about the work they're doing. Yet, the environments they work in are breath-taking. They appear to be separated from everything that is going on around them. They simply come to work, do the minimum they need to do, and then leave. It might be down to uninspiring leadership. When I do eventually get a full-time job, I want to work in a place where I feel excitement each day. A big part of that is being in a space where everyone feels like they can be themselves and have the freedom to be able to speak to

anyone and everyone. You want to be in an environment where no one's looked down upon, especially if they're a bit different. At my old school, everyone who works there – from the receptionists to the team leaders – are open with each other. They have direct conversations. Even the head teacher is very open. It's amazing. There's still a lot of pressure, but they are excited to be there, because it's a space where everyone can open up. There is no judgement. I hope this is replicated in the workplace that my generation enters.

What's your view on the importance that Generation Z, which is you and your friends, place on Pay and Purpose?
Ultimately, we live in a capitalist society. You need to make money to survive, so that's going to be a driving force for most people. But you should be able to be happy AND make money at the same time. For me personally – and my friends that I've spoken to about this – there must be something more than waking up and going to work to make money. You want to work for a purpose, even if it's just that the company supports local charities in some way. Over the last 6 months, a lot of businesses, especially in Peckham [a district in South London], want to get involved in the Peckham community. Gentrification is becoming a massive thing in Peckham, so they're trying to do something, to help provide a solution. Even just that angle of it gives workers more excitement. They connect with that purpose. They can recognise the impact that their business is making to their local community, or the world around them.

Just to turn it onto an external perspective, what makes you connect to a brand? What do you look for in a brand that would make you spend money with them?
I think that my generation is more interested in the environment. Every generation has been worried about these things, but it's just more pronounced for my generation. I am interested in brands that I know are conscious of this. The first thing on my mind is not always, "Are they environmentally conscious?" …. as a young student, the first thing I think of is the price of something, but I also want to know that I'm not contributing to some poor child working in a factory for a few pennies per day. I like brands doing something respectful, that can tie to the kind of person I am.

Finally, do you have a favourite 'quote' or motto or motto that you live your life by?
I have a lot, because I watch too many TV shows! So many of them end with moralistic one-liners! But recently, I had a conversation with someone who said their life motto is simply, "Because sometimes…" I love the idea of that being what guides her. When she thinks about what she wants to do in the future, she just thinks to herself "Because sometimes…" and [it] allows her to think about all the positives and negatives that come from that. I have borrowed her quote and have started using it myself! It is certainly making me reflect more on things.

Interview: CC

I want to work in a place where I feel excitement each day. A big part of that is being in a space where everyone feels like they can be themselves and have the freedom to be able to speak to anyone and everyone.

The CEO has to set very high levels of ambition and pace. If CEOs don't do this, their organisations slow down.

Tony Danker

POSITION AT TIME OF INTERVIEW:
Incoming Director General, Confederation of British Industry (CBI)

Tony Danker grew up in Belfast during the troubles, and moved to Manchester to study Law, aged 18. In the years that have followed, Tony's career has spanned both the public and private sectors, working for HM Treasury, and The Guardian, as well as completing his Masters in Public Administration at the Harvard Kennedy School. Tony also spent a number of years honing his consulting skills at McKinsey.

At the time of our interview, Tony was about to join the CBI, succeeding Dame Carolyn Fairbairn as its Director General. The CBI will play an important role in influencing the UK's long-term economic policy, post-Brexit, and post-COVID.

This is the only interview in our book that has taken place since the COVID-19 pandemic has struck. As the outgoing CEO of Be The Business – a not-for-profit movement helping business in the UK improve their productivity – and the incoming Director General of the CBI, Tony has spoken to hundreds of business leaders about the pandemic's effects on UK businesses.

Tony discusses his career, and the leadership lessons he has picked up during the COVID disruption.

You grew up in Belfast in the early '70s, during the troubles. As someone who grew up in London during the same period, and remembers the news being dominated by sectarian violence in Northern Ireland, I am interested to find out whether you have happy memories of your childhood?
I have very happy memories of childhood. I think it's only when I left Belfast for university when I was 18 that I realised there was something unusual about it. Back then I was disproportionately interested in the news, probably even more than I imagine you were! In Northern Ireland it centred around murder, political intrigue and constitutional change … and it was happening all around us. My neighbour was assassinated while we were having dinner one evening. I remember soldiers with guns inspecting the buses into town every day, and several times driving into riots and petrol bombs; but I was in no way traumatised by the events. It was our normal.

Am I right in thinking you started your career at McKinsey?
Long before McKinsey I spent spent a couple of years working for the then Chief Rabbi Jonathan Sacks, as a special adviser. That gave me an early taste for public life and leadership in a public role. After that, I worked at The Communication Group, a PR and lobbying firm. I went to McKinsey at 26.

McKinsey was a place where I did loads of different things. It allowed me to travel the world, gain my Masters, learn so much about business and strategy, and touch so many different industries. It was a brilliant foundation. I was very happy there until one day, a week after the Lehmann Brothers collapse, I got a call to go to the government.

I assume your capability at McKinsey had been spotted by some of the senior mandarins there, had you done a project there?
A week after Lehmann Brothers, the Prime Minister reorganised No. 10 to focus on the economic response to the crisis. The people I knew there from previous projects and university life thought that I could add a lot of value by joining the team.

Most of my work was designing the economic rescue package and then improving public sector efficiency. Within an hour of walking into No. 10 I was in meetings with well-known politicians working in 'crisis mode' to save the economy. That was hugely invigorating and prescient given recent events.

So, after that stint, what brought you to The Guardian?
I knew The Guardian commercial team from my work as a consultant, and the editorial team I had got to know during my time in government. I started off as a freelance consultant doing strategy work for the CEO at

the time, Andrew Miller. Soon that grew into developing The Guardian's international strategy.

I joined to help launch Guardian America and Guardian Australia. As the internationally-focused member of the ExCo, I started thinking less market-by-market ways to globalise The Guardian, but more in terms of developing global verticals. Eventually that migrated into global platform relationships. I developed working relationships with the likes of Google, Facebook, Apple, Twitter and so on.

Whilst The Guardian was, on one hand, in the legacy industry of print media, on the other, it was an incredibly ambitious digital organisation. So not only did I get to understand the commercial realities of the business, I had a great induction into the digital world.

You were the first CEO of Be the Business. Were you involved at the beginning of the conversation about this mission – helping UK businesses increase their productivity – or did the group approach you?
The original conversations surrounding Be the Business preceded me. Charlie Mayfield and Richard Lambert had gathered a group of leading businesspeople, FTSE chairs and CEOs, who had agreed with David Cameron and George Osborne that they would do a report into why UK productivity was so poor. After this report was published in 2016, the government immediately granted £13m in seed funding to set up a leading organisation focusing on productivity in the UK. I didn't know about this. The first I heard was when a head-hunter contacted me in March 2017 asking if I was interested in potentially becoming the CEO of this weird and wonderful thing. To me, 'CEO, weird and wonderful thing' was exactly what I felt I should be doing with my life at that stage.

I met Charlie and instantly was hooked. Charlie is one of the most inspiring people I have ever worked for; his passion and his belief in approaching this problem of national significance was amazing. I had never thought of launching a start-up. I didn't see myself as that guy … but this had *everything*. It was a brand-new start-up – with some money – and a board of the great and the good. It was public-spirited, but also focused on business performance. The only downside was that it didn't yet exist!

What were the leadership traits in Charlie Mayfield that made such an impression upon you?
He has a ton of integrity, he is deeply interested in people, and he is a leader-as-coach. Everything I bounced off him, he wanted it to be bolder and bigger. Charlie helped me learn that the CEO has to set very high levels of ambition and pace. If CEOs don't do this, their organisations slow down. Like me, Charlie is a dreamer. I found

that very infectious. Every time I was trying to be pragmatic and operational, Charlie pushed me to be more ambitious, be better, be faster. I think that had a direct consequence on the way I led the business and the way I now view leadership in general.

What types of British business leaders have impressed you over the last six months given the unprecedented change that we have experienced with the Coronavirus Pandemic?
At the beginning of the crisis, everybody had a wobble. Then, swiftly after, there was a huge surge in leadership confidence, in activism, and in command and control management. All of a sudden, leaders of SME and micro businesses became superhero CEOs, using a very traditional model of CEO leadership. They took 40 decisions in the space of two or three months, the likes of which they would take perhaps two or three per year in normal times. All of them had an adrenaline surge and moved their businesses to make changes far faster than before. It's the untold story of COVID really; this surge in leadership confidence and action by a set of business leaders who had greatness thrust upon them.

In our survey work we saw three years of innovation delivered in three months. We saw four times the rate of technology adoption in three months than the whole of last year. We have seen huge levels of decisiveness. However, the interesting thing has been as lockdown has ended and restarts have begun, things have become a lot more uncertain. There are a lot of very big decisions to be made once more but in an uncertain environment. Over the last three months (June – August 2020), staff engagement has waned. Now you have people with real resilience issues, mental health, lack of connectivity, lack of engagement with the business, all at a time where the CEO needs to squeeze margins. Restart is harder than lockdown. So, I think now is the hardest time to be a business leader.

I would say if you told me 6 months ago that we were about to see unprecedented levels of firms pursuing efficiency, innovation and technology I would have bitten your hand off. It's what the British economy has been missing for years; but it's tragic it has taken this crisis for that to happen.

What are some of the best interventions in terms of managing employee wellbeing during the COVID crisis?
One firm in the North West, with about 150 staff, hired an independent wellness support organisation to reach out to staff independent of management. They discovered a lot of their employees' mental health was being affected from being at home and not having work in their life. By having a caring and dedicated broker, they found the insights which led them to start thinking about engaging those on furlough with training and trying to bring people back to work.

Another one was a manufacturing business with a few hundred people. The CEO started to use Facebook Workplace to give a running dialogue, open to all. This helped to counterbalance the issues which arise from a command-and-control approach, using an engagement platform so people could debate and discuss easily.

A personal one on a smaller scale was an idea which one of my teams suggested to me. We replaced our regular 'lunch and learn' session with 'wine and wittering'. We had a glass of wine together on Zoom in a purpose made session for people to talk about the crisis, how it was affecting them, their friends, their workplaces, and how we thought it might be affecting our customers. I could not believe the impact these 'wine & wittering' sessions had, simply by allowing the workplace to be that community, that social space. It was a cathartic process. People wanted and needed to share this unprecedented experience.

Congratulations on your recent appointment as Director General Of the CBI. As its new leader you are being confronted with two of the biggest challenges imaginable. Notwithstanding a huge amount of change sweeping over the UK business due to COVID, what are some of the exciting things which businesses can potentially look forward to post-Brexit?

Whether you were 'for Brexit', or against it, one cannot argue that the pressing question it poses is how to grow the UK's competitiveness on a global stage for the next five years. During COVID, the biggest cliché has been that we want to 'build back better.' But, what does *build back better* actually mean? To me, it doesn't just mean let's get back to levels of demand which were true in February 2020. It means setting ourselves up to be globally thriving by 2025.

Britain must have an actionable economic strategy. The truth is that successful economies – particularly those which have recently left a trading block – have established a national economic strategy. With that in mind, I believe the business community is best placed to set out this national economic strategy. I think the notion that we are handed economic strategy by politicians is completely wrong. The role I believe the CBI should play is articulating with, and on behalf of, British business to create a very exciting, high growth, competitive strategy for the future of the country.

I would like to finish our discussion by asking you to offer some advice for recent university and college leavers, who are making their first tentative steps into the world of work. What advice would you give to those who are at the beginning of their careers, facing significant disruption to their vocation and employment?
We don't yet know what this generation will be like. The millennial generation has had something of a bad press. They combine all the superpowers of being autonomous, socially ambitious and highly digital, with an occasional sense of entitlement.

But the truth is the most successful millennials have not felt entitled but have felt empowered. They have brought all their superpowers to be amongst the best generation of young leaders we have ever seen. After recent events, for better or for worse, the next generation maybe won't have that same sense of entitlement. But I hope they have that same level of supercharged skill and appetite, and to some degree self-belief. We should hope they can be the perfect blend of being the most super-equipped generation we have seen in terms of being leaders in companies, but also being hugely conscientious and collaborative.

To me, the most important thing is that they are eager to participate in the collective endeavour of building great companies. Charlie Mayfield has a phrase for work which I have always loved – 'work is a place which we get in and get on in life'. I think that is probably the greatest social role that companies can play. I think that should remain the contract between us and this next generation of employees.

Interview: OP (London)

The most successful millennials have not felt entitled but have felt empowered. They have brought all their superpowers to be amongst the best generation of young leaders we have ever seen.

'Here comes the sun, here comes the sun, it's alright.'

— George Harrison, The Beatles

QUARTER FIVE

Our Clairvoyance

Looking forward

2020 will be remembered as a capricious and disconcerting year for many public sector leaders and private business proprietors alike.

At the time of this book's publication, the Coronavirus Pandemic continues to rip through society, discriminating against older generations and those with underlying health issues. It has caused widespread mental anguish to school and college-aged students who have had their educational experiences seriously impacted.

Some leaders have disappointed - or appeared lacklustre at best - revealing that their dominant leadership mode hitherto has mostly been 'management by numbers' and 'like-for-likes', rather fostering a culture of reinvention and evolution.

Of course, some industry sectors have also been desperately unlucky. Travel, leisure and hospitality have been left in a perilous state. Fashion retail has been battered. The Arts sector has been dealt a hammer blow.

There are other leaders – not to mention a cohort of emerging superstars – who are showing real dynamism, clarity of purpose, profound compassion and forward-thinking. This provides us with hope and optimism.

We will return to some semblance of normality in time; even if the laboratories fail to find a vaccine, with other medical interventions, we will continue to adapt and learn to live with COVID. Society has done so with pandemics throughout the ages.

It is important to look forward.

At Q5, we spend the last hour of each week hosting what we jocularly refer to as "clairvoyant sessions." We invite a couple of industry chiefs to join us via Zoom. Together we channel our inner powers of prophecy and attempt to draw out pictures of what we think the future holds for their sector.

- What might the world look like when we eventually emerge from the Pandemic, as we undoubtedly will?
- What might it mean for us as individuals?
- What might it mean for the way that we interact, travel, communicate in the future?
- How might it impact the way that we work (together and with our clients) in the years ahead?
- How will it affect the many industry sectors we support?

Everyone has found the instinctive process of shaping the future to be fun, and a welcome distraction from lockdown living, and as a result the Clairvoyant sessions have been an uplifting experience for our guests, as well as our Q5 colleagues.

Of course, the major problem with leadership is short-termism. CEOs, often on three-year contracts, tend to therefore think in three-year cycles; review the as-is, set out a future course and pray for a return in year 3. Most Governmental leaders struggle to look beyond their parliamentary tenure.

But if one looks forward to 2030, we think the coming years will provide some huge opportunities:

- **Digital has proved it can rule the roost.** Those businesses that have only modestly invested in digital channels have seized the opportunity through the Pandemic to reduce their physical footprint, and re-pivot their businesses to be part of the 'mobile' future.
- **A lot of empty retail and office space has come available**. Entrepreneurial leaders will continue to rapidly think through new ways to re-purpose this space. We predict that the 2020s will be a golden age for entrepreneurs, who are bold and courageous.
- **Teams have proved that they can be based anywhere.** For professional services firms, this has been an epiphany. The same for lawyers. There is no longer a need to congregate in one place. Many professionals can carry out their work from anywhere.
- **'Silver surfers' are continuing to wield vast spending power, but online.** Over 65s have had to get used to shielding and reducing social contact until an effective COVID-19 vaccine is found. This will continue to provide enterprising businesses with a massive opportunity to serve the needs of cash-rich (and bored) Baby Boomers.

We look forward to sharing stories of those clever ideas that turn into global successes - and of course those that fall asunder too – in Volume 2.

Acknowledgements

First and foremost, we would like to thank everyone who was interviewed for Magic Sponge. Without their contributions and commitment, this book would never have been produced. Without our interviewees, we would have been left with a series of bland, unanswered questions.

Thank you to Sharon Rice-Oxley, Chris Parsons, Daryl Edwards and Carla Schaeffer for co-founding Q5 with me. Back in 2009, we probably didn't appreciate that our decision to build a consulting firm would give us access to such an extraordinary and eclectic mix of business leaders. Daryl also kindly wrote the prefaces that open each Quarter of this book.

Thank you to Andy Cottrill and Tom Leary, who joined Q5 in years two and three respectively and have contributed to this collection of interviews.

A debt of gratitude is also owed to some other key interviewers including Jen Gramolt, Dan Upward and Chris Conder.

Thank you to Clare Burton, who provided much needed project management support, cracking the whip on more than one occasion.

Thank you to Neil Kerber for contributing witty, thoughtful illustrations.

Thank you to Andrew Dunn, James Carey and Sarah Pyke, who fortunately know a thing or two about publishing and whose guidance helped us deliver something that is half palatable.

Thank you to Sophie Powell Cook and Alice Pearson, for their sterling efforts in transcribing and sub-editing so many of the interviews, and to Ethan Kline for proof-reading with aplomb.

We would like to thank our clients over the last ten years for daring to engage us and, of course, our Q5 colleagues over the years, for their passion, energy and commitment to the cause.

Thank you, dear reader, for taking possession of this book. You probably weren't given an option to decline it. All the same, we hope you enjoy it.

OP